T0159101

# PARENTING
## *from*
# WHOLENESS

Ten Habits for Bringing Out the Best in Your Child

## CAROLE E. GAECKLE

Foreword by Jillian Sullivan, PhD

**BALBOA.**
PRESS

A DIVISION OF HAY HOUSE

Copyright © 2016 Carole E. Gaeckle.

All rights reserved. No part of this book may be used or reproduced by any means, graphic, electronic, or mechanical, including photocopying, recording, taping or by any information storage retrieval system without the written permission of the author except in the case of brief quotations embodied in critical articles and reviews.

Balboa Press books may be ordered through booksellers or by contacting:

Balboa Press
A Division of Hay House
1663 Liberty Drive
Bloomington, IN 47403
www.balboapress.com
1 (877) 407-4847

Because of the dynamic nature of the Internet, any web addresses or links contained in this book may have changed since publication and may no longer be valid. The views expressed in this work are solely those of the author and do not necessarily reflect the views of the publisher, and the publisher hereby disclaims any responsibility for them.

The author of this book does not dispense medical advice or prescribe the use of any technique as a form of treatment for physical, emotional, or medical problems without the advice of a physician, either directly or indirectly. The intent of the author is only to offer information of a general nature to help you in your quest for emotional and spiritual well-being. In the event you use any of the information in this book for yourself, which is your constitutional right, the author and the publisher assume no responsibility for your actions.

Any people depicted in stock imagery provided by Thinkstock are models, and such images are being used for illustrative purposes only. Certain stock imagery © Thinkstock.

Print information available on the last page.

ISBN: 978-1-5043-4484-5 (sc)
ISBN: 978-1-5043-4485-2 (e)

Library of Congress Control Number: 2015918715

Balboa Press rev. date: 2/12/2016

# Contents

Foreword ............................................................................ vii

Preface ................................................................................ xi

Dedication ......................................................................... xiii

Introduction ........................................................................ xv

Chapter 1:  Preparing for the Climb
            *Set Your Intentions* ........................................... 1

Chapter 2:  Parenting Decisions
            *Choose Consciously* ........................................... 5

Chapter 3:  It Is *All* about You ... It Is *Not* about You
            *Embrace Detachment and Objectivity* ........... 15

Chapter 4:  Tell Me the Truth—Even When
            It Is Hard to Say and Hear
            *The Value of Truth* .......................................... 29

Chapter 5:  Feeling Special ... Just Like Everyone Else
            *A Soul to Soul Connection* ............................. 41

Chapter 6:  Greatest Strength ... Greatest Weakness
            *The Real Value of a Trait* .............................. 55

Chapter 7:  You Make Such Good Decisions ...
            What Were You Thinking?
            *Learning What You Do Want* ....................69

Chapter 8:  Completely Involved ... Letting Go
            *What You Focus on Expands* ....................81

Chapter 9:  Will This Never End ...
            Where Did the Time Go?
            *Enjoy the Climb* ....................95

Chapter 10: Beyond the Summit ... Perils and Joys
            *Letting Go of the Outcome* .................... 105

Afterword.................................................... 119
A Brief Summary of Mount Everest .................... 121
Acknowledgments........................................123
Notes .........................................................125
References....................................................127
About the Author........................................... 131

# Foreword

What a great book you are about to embark upon! The author has a special skill for identifying and promoting some of the most optimal courses of development, especially those of self-discipline and self-regulation. I was frequently struck with the amount of research that supports the concepts discussed in this book. Parenting books often ignore these aspects, but as a researcher into these concepts, I can tell you that they are easily the number-one predictor of success and very much protective against a huge range of mental and physical illnesses. 1-3*

The chance that your child will say no to smoking or drugs in the face of peer pressure, for example, depends on her ability to overcome temptation with the knowledge that it will be a bad decision in the long-term. As you can probably guess thinking back to your child when she was just a baby, humans are not born with good self-regulation; the infant or toddler cries when she is unhappy, pulls the computer cords even though she knows she is not allowed to, and pokes her fingers into the birthday cake before the song is complete. Instead, self-regulation develops with time, and indeed the front-most areas of the brain orchestrating this ability are not fully mature until the mid-twenties, which is why you will continue to be dismayed with some of your child's poor judgments throughout her teenage years. This book highlights the importance of providing a strong self-regulation foundation and provides numerous strategies for enhancing self-regulation in your child. What really sets this book apart from other parenting books is the emphasis on the parent rather than the child. We often forget that children watch and absorb their parents' insecurities and defense mechanisms into their own personalities. Our own reactions to our children's actions are sometimes more important than the lesson we are trying to teach them. Self-regulation is therefore important to cultivate in yourself as a parent as well, as this book describes throughout. If you overreact emotionally to your child's poor behavior, you are likely to act controlling or say something you will later regret, as described in chapter 3, but if you can reappraise and control your feelings, you will be better able to calmly assess, reflect, and sensitively guide your child. Even responding compassionately to your child depends on your own self-regulation; if you are greatly distressed and cannot control your negative emotions when you see your child in pain, it will result in a self-focus and inability to help or empathize with her 8*. Studies have shown greater parental sensitivity to be associated with better social and emotional development in their children 9-11*, while a childhood with more intrusive or controlling parents is associated with higher rates of physical and mental health problems 12*.

All this requires proactive and careful reflection on the parents' part, and this book repeatedly discusses the importance of a planned approach to parenting by asking questions rather than simply telling you what to do. The author highlights the importance of knowing your own strengths and weaknesses (as well as those in your child) without necessarily criticizing them and using these to guide your parenting journey. A field that is becoming increasingly popular in neuroscience is that of mindfulness training, *mindfulness* being defined as a deliberate state of nonjudgmental awareness of your feelings and the world around you. Studies have shown that training in this meditation-related technique is associated with many benefits, including the ability to cope under stress, better health, greater compassion, and even showing brain growth in areas associated with learning, memory, and self-regulation 17-19*.

While there are certainly no real answers to child rearing, and as the author repeatedly stresses, they differ greatly between children and families, having an open and reflective attitude and promoting self-discipline and self-regulation is going to lead you far in your parenting journey. I hope you enjoy the book as much as I did!

Jillian Sullivan, PhD
University of Cambridge

\* References for these studies provided in the back of the book.

# Preface

This book is a summary of knowledge gathered along my path regarding how to improve my parenting and how to be a better person. I have been blessed by many mentors. Much of my life has entailed work with and around children and parents. I am not a doctor in the field. I am a parent. And I have a talent of compiling good information, figuring out how to make it practical, and sharing it with others. This book is the result of many years spent collecting, honing, testing, and experiencing great ideas in parenting.

*To the best in each of us.*

# Introduction

After college, I worked at a juvenile detention facility where I frequently found myself bewildered by parenting behaviors, wondering what they were thinking. I encountered parents who delayed the uncomfortable conversation and then placed adoption articles around the home so their teenager would "figure it out." There were parents who picked their daughter up from completing alcohol rehabilitation and then stopped at the liquor store for a few celebratory beers. The result: their child returned to detention without ever making it home. And then there were the parents who turned a blind eye to the bike stealing ring their young sons set up in the garage. Oh, it is so easy to judge from the outside!

Once I became a parent, I began to understand the incredible challenges parents encounter. This is not to condone inappropriate choices. It is to acknowledge that as parents we often make mistakes, even when our goals are well-meaning. Much of parenting falls into a gray, hazy paradox where confusion and frustration reside. We end up spewing old ideas from our parents—things we swore we would never do. We rant, scream, say unkind things, walk away from responsibilities, and become horrified by some of our thoughts and behaviors.

We desperately want to do a good job. So what happens? The bottom line is it takes more than just wanting to raise a happy, healthy, successful child. It requires lifting the cloud of contradictions by becoming aware of our thoughts. It involves learning how to embrace our emotions, love ourselves, and take responsibility for our lives. It requires a deep reservoir of courage. And it entails real acceptance of the innate wisdom, wonder, and capacity of our children.

Whether conscious of it or not, each of us has preconceived ideas about the kind of parent we want to be. We formulate expectations of our children. These thoughts have implications. They create an inner guidance system that can help or hinder maneuvering the many unexpected twists and turns associated with parenting. By examining these preconceived ideas, we can develop the relationship we truly desire with our children.

Sound impossible or daunting? In truth, you already use these skills to some extent. Consider the process of buying a car. When you do some research, review ratings, ask others how they like their vehicles, and/or take a few test drives, your satisfaction greatly improves. The same basic process is true for parenting. When you clearly consider what you want to create and the optimal plan for success, your results improve.

Whether you are just beginning the journey or are well into the adventure, this book will help you contemplate the common ambiguities parents face and assess your thoughts and expectations. Consider what the terms *good parent*, *happy child*, and *successful adult* mean. What parameters do you want to set for your child? What relationship do you want your child to have with the world? Thinking through these things will provide you with guideposts for gaining clarity, confidence, and courage in your parenting. And it will offer guidance on how to honor your child's essence.

Some concepts may seem uncomfortable. You may not agree with each idea. That is okay! But do yourself a favor. If you reach a point that does not resonate with you, don't chuck it. Stack it on a mental shelf and return to it later—maybe next week, maybe next year. Your child's developmental stage may have changed by then, and the concept be of value to you. Whether you agree or disagree, the pages will encourage you to think, reexamine your own beliefs and experiences, and formulate a clearer picture of the most important role you'll ever accept—being a parent.

The following list will be helpful to know as you read and begin this journey:

- The goal is to inspire a soul-to-soul connection with your child.
- Each chapter begins with an analogy to climbing Mount Everest.*
  - It offers a concrete example of the concept to be introduced.
  - It encourages a summit-view perspective of the relationship you hope to achieve with your child.
- The pronouns he and she are used alternately.
- Anecdotes used are a compilation of parenting in general. Any relation to specific individuals or circumstances is coincidental. These examples are set off from the main text.
- The structure concentrates on concepts versus chronology.
- The concepts apply to all developmental stages.

Becoming a perfect parent or raising a perfect child is an unrealistic goal. Give yourself a break. Instead, work toward consistently showing up as the ever-improving, best version of yourself. Continuously learn. Be gentle with yourself. Have compassion for your fellow parents.

I wish you all the best on your parenting journey!

Carole E. Gaeckle

* A brief summary of Mount Everest can be found in the back of the book.

CHAPTER 1

---

# Preparing for the Climb

## *Set Your Intentions*

When Sir Edmund Hillary and Tenzing Norgay reached the summit of Mount Everest in May 1953, it was after years of climbing experience and planning. They did not just put on their boots one day and decide to climb the mountain. They were part of an organized four hundred-person team of porters, guides, and climbers. The necessary food, gear, and weather and the slow, steady pace of high-altitude acclimation all factored into their success. The feat was life threatening, but the result was life changing.

Because parenting is not typically life threatening, we seldom undertake the kind of preparation required for climbing Mount Everest. However, most of us agree that parenting is the most important job in the world. Would a little more planning and preparation be beneficial? Would it make the journey more enriching and the outcomes more rewarding? Would we feel more capable of handling the daunting task and more likely to press on when the challenge before us seems overwhelming? Would we navigate the bumps in the road more confidently if we took the time to think about the type of parent we want to be, the type of parents we were raised by, and the type of long-term relationship we want to have with our child? What if we viewed parenting as a journey instead of a destination?

Parents provide the basics: food, shelter, and clothing. Beyond that, the roads diverge. Are parents also responsible for extracurricular activities, moral upbringing, or self-esteem? If so, for how long? What about how to parent? Is it imperative to *always* be the authority, or is it more important to indulge the child's sense of free expression? Is balance the goal?

Often we ask an expectant parent, "Is it a boy or a girl?" The better questions might be: What is your expectation of this child? What does having a boy or girl conjure up in your mind? Are you imagining an athlete, an intellectual, a musician, or a companion with whom you can shop or golf? What if you are hoping for a frilly girl and your child is a tomboy? What if you're anticipating a jock and instead he is into cooking?

We usually just admit to wanting our child to be happy and successful. But what is success or happiness? Is it becoming a doctor, lawyer, pianist, or Olympian? And are these goals his—or yours? What if your child enjoys activities completely different from your own? You like to fish, but he prefers to spend time drawing. What if your child aspires to be a body piercer or a rafting guide? In addition to wondering whether she will be able to support herself, you may question how society will view her. Be truthful—you may also wonder what your child's outcome ultimately says about you as a parent.

In parenting we are confronted with the mirror of our own insecurities, inadequacies, and societal conditioning. Our responses are often knee-jerk instead of insightful. What kind of parent do you want to be? Where are you currently operating? Close the gap by thinking before you act.

Ask yourself: What is the lifelong relationship I envision having with my child? Will you be his friend, his boss, his advocate, a protector, a mentor? If you want your child to become self-reliant, it is your job to work yourself out of a job—to teach him how to parent himself. Your child will have the opportunity for many friendships, but few will take the time to teach him how to make quality decisions, how to listen to his own instincts, how to nurture himself, how to forgive himself, and how to challenge himself to reach his potential. That is *your* job opportunity!

Planning and preparation are essential for the summit of Mount Everest. The expedition needs to continually adapt to the environment, assess expectations, and manage options. The same is true of parenting. Consider the timing; the availability of a support system; and the physical, emotional, and financial demands. Examine your expectations of yourself and how you impose those onto your child. Allow your decisions and choices to reflect the relationship you want to have with your child. Thoughtful intentions and actions will set you on a rewarding trek.

Ponder the journey and then … prepare for the climb of a lifetime!

CHAPTER 2

# Parenting Decisions

## Choose Consciously

In addition to the financial and time considerations, choosing to climb Mount Everest involves physical conditioning and a willingness to be exposed to extreme environmental conditions. It requires courage and flexibility to face ever-changing, even unexpected circumstances. Mental fortitude and a strong desire to succeed are essential.

Likewise, parenting requires incredible endurance, patience, and mental fortitude. It involves exposure to sleep deprivation, being covered in your child's body fluids, and, at times, a complete lack of personal space and time. Nothing can truly prepare you for the exhaustion and the sense of being overwhelmed, both by the magnitude of your responsibility and the magnitude of your ability to love. There are times of immense joy and fulfillment entwined with times of fear, fatigue, and overload. Amid it all, the biggest challenge is maintaining your resolve and commitment to succeed, because becoming a parent dramatically alters your life. Twenty-one-plus years is a major commitment.

Look within yourself and determine how you feel about being a parent and how you feel about your life in general. Have you made conscious choices, or are you simply going along the path you feel you have been handed? An exploration of your own life helps reveal how you feel about your child and about being a parent. Are you holding tightly to your old life? Have you welcomed the new addition and begun honoring the sacred new life? Were you thrilled with the idea of having a child but are now completely overwhelmed with the reality?

While it is important to create time for yourself, carve out time with your partner, and maintain some of your old friendships, having a child disrupts the status quo. It is okay to grieve the loss of your old life. It is important to make room for and embrace the new. Even if this is your second or third child, each addition stretches the old paradigm. New expectations and discussions are needed regarding responsibilities, chores, and daily obligations. Your child's arrival naturally raises new personal feelings of inadequacy. It requires a constant balancing act of your time and energy.

## Partners in Parenting

Is there a partner in your life? And if so, how involved is that person in your child's life? Have you discussed how your partner feels about being a parent? What adjustment is your partner going through? A parenting partner is a valuable resource. That person can be the sounding board when you need to vent, hear yourself think, or have a reality check. And in those

really difficult moments, your partner can help you maintain your perspective, offer reinforcement, and be a comfort.

On the flipside, having a child can cause real strain on your relationship with your partner. You and your partner may have different viewpoints on child rearing or levels of tolerance for various behaviors. Is it okay for your three-year-old to eat dessert before dinner or for your six-year-old to stay up until midnight? Is walking in the rain without an umbrella acceptable? Is it okay for your son to leave his wet towel on the floor? Can your daughter be fifteen minutes late after curfew? How many lost cell phones are excusable? Discuss the behaviors in terms of the level of importance and the personal impact on each of you. Be willing to contemplate options. Together, consider which behaviors are most significant, and for those, develop a unified front. On the minor issues, allow the different perspectives to illustrate to your child that there is more than one way to accomplish a task or view the world.

Does one parent take on the full responsibility for how things are to be accomplished? This can be a heavy burden. The weight of this responsibility can cause resentment. Does the other parent feel left out and bitter? Work toward compromise. For instance:

> The boys' bath time was about getting in, getting clean, and getting out—the quicker, the less mess, the better. For my partner, it was a time of fun and games—bubbles one night, squirt guns the next—water everywhere. It caused tension. I thought it was taking too long, making too much of a mess. I stood in the bathroom doorway, ready to speak my mind again. Then suddenly I was able to see the smiles stretched across my

sons' faces. Their belly laughter filled my ears. I realized my partner's way had real value. I needed to let go, to trust my partner. We did discuss maintaining bedtime and for the mess to be cleaned up by those making the mess. But from then on, bath time was my partner's arena. The result: my sons gained precious memories, my partner gained confidence, and I enjoyed some free time!

If you tend to take everything on, loosen up. Develop an open attitude that allows you to consider alternative options. Trust your partner. If you are the one who feels left out and wants to be heard, instead of deferring the decisions, be supportive while offering your perspective. Respect each other's viewpoints. Develop an attitude of gratitude. And definitely, definitely keep a sense of humor!

You and your partner both genuinely want to do a good job of raising your child. You both have fears of failing and of being inadequate. You each have ideologies based on how you were raised. Take time to listen to each other. Discuss the larger view of the relationship you want to cultivate with your child. Respect each other's needs and perspectives. Support one another. Work toward reaching consensus. Keep the lines of communication open.

What if we were to willingly listen to one another with the awareness that we each see the world in unique ways?[1]

—Margaret Wheatley

Parenting is a challenging endeavor, even more so if you are a single parent. Keep in mind it is normal to have moments when you feel overwhelmed or have self-doubts. Be gentle with yourself. Be open to seeking outside assistance from extended family, neighbors, church, or community resources.

Separation or divorce can offer another set of challenges. Regardless of the relationship status with your ex, when the two of you have a child, your former partner remains a part of your life. Work diligently to maintain a respectful relationship and keep an open dialogue. Just as you feel every scrape your child endures, your child feels every barb you hurl at your ex. Regardless of the fact your child may be upset with the other parent, it is still his dad or mom. If trust has been broken between you and your ex, then it may be more difficult to have trust in that person's parenting decisions. Even if you were still together, there would be differences in parenting styles. Work toward seeing the value these differences might provide your child. And at the very least, honor the fact that this person plays an important part in your child's life, even if the person is physically absent.

## Who Is Minding Baby?

Who will be responsible for the day-to-day care of your child: the traditional stay-at-home mother, the stay-at-home dad, the small in-home day care, the large commercial day care, grandparents, or nannies? This is a complex decision. You will probably struggle with whatever choice you make. Considerations include: financial necessities, the earning power of each partner, individual emotional or physical needs, whether you have a partner, and what childcare options are available in your community. The choice is very personal, because circumstances are unique for each family.

Is your desire to stay home based on your upbringing? Are your philosophical views or your partner's travel schedule a factor in the equation? What opportunities does your community offer regarding playgroups or volunteer options? Do you instead long to go back to work because of the personal satisfaction your career brings? If so, what is the value you receive from working? Is it the social camaraderie, sense of purpose, or excelling up the ranks of management? Does your company offer telecommuting or flextime? Have you considered starting a home-based business?

Making this decision can be difficult. Living it is often even tougher. You may initially feel certain you want to stay home with your child, only to discover your financial situation changes or you need the social interaction of the workplace. Sometimes the realities of your selection look different than imagined. There is no wrong answer. It is okay to reevaluate your decision and change your mind. Analyze your individual situation. Decide what is best for you and your family. There are pros and cons to either choice.

If you choose to be a stay-at-home parent and primary caregiver, you will be extremely involved in your child's daily activities. You will have the opportunity to marvel at the incremental changes in your child's growth and relish the joys and intimacy of forming a strong bond. On the other hand, the tedium of the daily schedule may cause you to feel incredibly lonely, mentally unchallenged, or bored. You may miss the validation of a paycheck or the simple hello from coworkers. You may fear becoming unimportant as your career opportunities slip away. You may worry you are not doing it right, given the pressure that parenting is your job. Or you may feel overwhelmed at the magnitude of your job. You may begrudge picking up the volunteering slack of working parents or experience jealousy as working parents climb the ladder of success. You may feel you are superior because you elected to sacrifice your career in order to be responsible, but resentful society does not offer tangible validation.

If you return to work, you will maintain your professional identity. You will receive validation in the form of a paycheck, promotions, and social interactions. On the other hand, you will miss out on the daily events and incremental changes in your child's life. There may be challenges regarding consistent, quality childcare options or the value of the information you receive from your childcare provider. You may feel guilty when your child acts out and wonder if you are failing to fully bond with your child. You may feel you are always juggling your time, being pulled in two directions, never feeling like you are doing anything well, or constantly grieving all the missed moments. You may feel indignant at the stay-at-home parent's request for you to volunteer, adding to your overly full plate. Or you may feel defensive of the judgment you sense when you decline volunteering. You may dismiss the stay-at-home parent's work as easier or less valid to a household's success. You may consider the stay-at-home parent as less intelligent, out-of-touch, or unwilling to make the sacrifices for success.

Either way, the choice is tough. Both sides justify their decisions and placate the virtues of the other. The working parent may acknowledge that the stay-at-home parent has the hardest job in the world while at the same time thinking the parent does not have the same burden or pressure level and is therefore not quite as sophisticated or capable. And while the stay-at-home parent is acknowledging the incredible stress the working parent is under to juggle career and home, may also be thinking the working parent is selfish and irresponsible or less capable and neglectful regarding home life. When resentment builds, both judge the other based on their own internal fears, inadequacies, and jealousies. Whatever you choose, keep in mind most working parents spend quality time with their children. Many devote numerous hours to volunteering. Most stay-at-home parents remain motivated and intelligent. They may also be serving in leadership positions in the community, on school boards, or within nonprofit organizations. Honor your personal decision and trust and respect the decisions of other parents. By consciously facing and accepting your own choices, you reduce the need to justify your decision, blame your child, hold guilt over your partner, or even blindly maintain your current path. You empower yourself and thereby open your ability to empower your child.

Also consider that by supporting rather than resenting one another, you can develop a sense of community for yourself and your child. Offer to include the working parent's child in your carpool or playgroup or to give the stay-at-home parent's high school student career guidance or an internship. By embracing one another's choices, you can create a win-win for yourself and your child.

Mount Everest climber Beck Weathers, in his book *Left for Dead*, discusses what it takes for high-altitude climbing:

> It takes a lot of effort and mental maturity to climb a big hill. It is not something you do on natural gifts alone. You've got to learn the skills. High-altitude climbers must enjoy putting themselves in situations where they're not sure how they're going to respond…No matter how

good you are, you're never sure you can do it. You're testing yourself. You hope you will be honorable, that you won't fall apart, that you'll maintain, that your courage won't desert you, that you'll give fully of what you have. But you don't know until the moment of truth. At some level you fear that when tested you'll prove a person of little character, nothing but a coward.[2]

Parenting also requires maturity—the ability to put another person's needs and desires before your own. It entails being responsible for yourself, as well as the day in, day out safety and growth of your child. Parenting is relentless, time-consuming, and costly. It involves years of effort and perseverance and of facing your own personal anxiety, self-doubts, and fears. It necessitates developing new skills and new levels of self-control. It involves making personal sacrifices. It can strain even the strongest of partnerships. At the same time, if you have the courage and fortitude to see it through, you will be in awe as you watch your child's development. You will grow tremendously as a person. And you will be treating yourself to an incredibly rewarding, enriching, and joyous experience!

## CHAPTER 3

# It Is *All* about You ... It Is *Not* about You

### *Embrace Detachment and Objectivity*

Mount Everest guides are responsible for preparation and leadership, including sharing vital information with members of the team. Their wisdom and abilities are essential. It is also important for each individual on the team to be mindful of their own particular abilities and limitations. They need awareness regarding how their personal bodies are responding to the challenging conditions. They need to assess how strong the leader is performing and how well the team is functioning as a unit. Each of the individuals is ultimately accountable for their own experience.

As a parent, you are responsible for guiding your child, providing safety and security, and imparting wisdom to the best of your ability. Your child is also accountable for the decisions she makes and for the thoughts and actions she chooses. The challenge is that the lines between your responsibilities and those of your child are sometimes blurred, sometimes clear.

She got into the private preschool because you showed up at four o'clock in the morning to stand in line for registration. She earned a spot on the basketball team because she practiced for hours every day. When things do not go as planned, it may feel like it is your fault—if only you had warned her, pushed her to study harder, or forced yourself to have the difficult conversations. The lines can seem fuzzy. Her pain is your pain when she is bullied, fails a test, or is rejected by a friend. It can feel overwhelming, heart wrenching.

In real life there is no crystal ball. Your child does not come with a personal manual, though you may often wish she did! During the first five years of her life, you and the other role models in her life *are* her manual.

> What you do speaks so loudly that I cannot hear what you say.
>
> —Ralph Waldo Emerson

She memorizes your every nuance, and when she starts to play back the tape, you may not always be happy with the performance. Is she reflecting the emotions you are feeling that day, demonstrating a behavior you are embarrassed to admit you possess, or just leaving you wondering where you went wrong? These moments are an opportunity for her personal growth, especially if you are willing to see her as a separate individual with her own path. Consider this poet's words:

> Your children are not your children.
> They are the sons and daughters
> of Life's longing for itself.
> They come through you but not from you,

And though they are with you,
yet they belong not to you.
You may give them your love
but not your thoughts.
For they have their own thoughts.
You may house their bodies but not their souls,
For their souls dwell in the house
of tomorrow, which you cannot
visit, not even in your dreams.
You may strive to be like them, but
seek not to make them like you.
For life goes not backward nor
tarries with yesterday.
You are the bows from which your
children as living arrows are sent forth.
The archer sees the mark upon the path of
the infinite, and He bends you with His
might that His arrows may go swift and far.
Let your bending in the archer's
hand be for gladness;
For even as He loves the arrow that flies,
so He loves also the bow that is stable.[3]

—Khalil Gibran

Just as your child needs your wisdom and guidance, she also needs to value herself as a separate, unique being—to recognize she is a soul with her own journey. You help create this space by seeing beyond her face, beyond her pain or joy, and into the essence of her being. Accept her individuality. Honor her spirit. Reinforce her independence, even when her vision is in conflict with the vision you have for her.

## Life Is Theater

Think for a moment about watching a play. You may develop empathy for the characters. You feel as if you completely understand what a character is going through and experiencing. From the audience perspective, you see all the factors influencing the character, even ones the character is unaware of. You may find yourself wanting to tell the character to watch out for that conniving scoundrel, to listen to the friend telling her the truth, or to relax because it's all going to work out, but you know you are just watching a play. Part of you is detached. You do not feel responsible for the actions or outcomes of the characters. You know that when the play is over you will leave the theater. That same sense of detachment is a beneficial tool in parenting.

Certainly embrace the moments when your child is feeling joyous, loving—giving you a hug. Soak it in fully. When your child is acting like a wild, irrational person, agitated, or even cruel, allow your perspective to switch to that of an audience member. Observe the behavior while avoiding the pull to take it personally.

How do you attain a detached perspective? It is challenging, especially with people you love. Check in with yourself. What are you feeling? What is your fear? Take a deep breath. In your mind, visualize moving into the theater chair while you watch your child on the stage. Ask yourself: What is this really about? What else do I need to understand? Remind yourself that her behavior is about something, someone, or an unmet need—her disappointing soccer game, the argument with her brother, or a lack of sleep. All of these things may have little or nothing to do with you personally. Even if it does involve you personally, your detachment will aid you in a more appropriate response.

Developing objectivity is also easier if you maintain a clear vision of your role as a parent. Is it your job to mold your child—coax her into the person you think she needs to become? Is your role to support her in cultivating her own vision? Do you feel a need to remove all her imperfections, make her learn to behave, or persuade her to excel in certain ways? Parents often say: "I want what is best for my child." In reality, the line between wanting your child to be the best *she can be* and be what *you expect* her to be can get murky. You have a program in your head about what behaviors, lifestyles, clothing, and attitudes are acceptable. How you impose those on your child affects your relationship. It affects how your child views herself.

Would your life be different if someone had made you feel completely accepted and loved when you were young, regardless of your behavior? What would have been the impact if someone had helped you understand that your life was really important, just because you existed? Would it have changed anything if you were permitted to express the fact that you were upset because it meant you were voicing your uniqueness or bringing awareness to an unspoken problem?

This is in no way to suggest that you condone ruthless or harmful behaviors. It is simply stepping back mentally and emotionally. Instead of attempting to control your child by ridiculing or forcing her, be open to understanding how she came to her behavior. Help her examine potential alternatives. What if instead of thinking of your child as someone to *change*, you have a curiosity about how she sees the world—as if she is a foreign exchange student completely unfamiliar with your culture and norms. You seek to examine and review things with her. You look to learn as much from her as she learns from you.

## Where's the Logic?

As adults, we have an assortment of emotions. Feelings are our indicator lights. They let us know something is going on. Your child will also have a variety of emotions, some of which you may deem irrational! Accept all of her feelings, including the highly charged, seemingly unreasonable ones. Realize outbursts are especially common when your child wants things to be different from the current reality—for her favorite cereal not to be all gone, to be out of the car during a long drive, or for her dad to visit as he promised. Instead of responding with logic, it is often more helpful to say, "I wish I could twitch my nose and make it happen for you." Sometimes that is all it takes to calm her emotions. She wants to know you are on her side. She needs to know you heard her and you care.

While all emotions are acceptable, some behaviors are intolerable. Reflect on your views regarding discipline. Is it ever okay to spank? Do you interpret the phrase, "Spare the rod, spoil the child," to mean if you spank, you will avoid creating a spoiled child? Or are you supposed to avoid spanking and instead need to spoil the child? Is the rod referring to a shepherd's staff used to guide sheep, and therefore, you are called to guide your child? What is effective discipline? Is it punishment or humiliation? Or is it helping your child understand the significance of her actions and examine alternative solutions?

When your child misbehaves, consider your overall objective in the situation. Be aware of the frustration, embarrassment, or inadequacy you may be feeling. Help your child understand the benefits of the desired behavior. In some circumstances, time-outs may allow your child the opportunity to calm down. Whenever possible, instill the desire to want to behave. It is much more powerful than any external discipline. An example:

One moment Trevor was playing nicely, and the next he was throwing sand in his friend's face. I was horrified. As the friend began to cry, his mom's face shone with rage. Internally, I wanted to scream at and even shake my child. I wanted to run and hide. I was furious, embarrassed. I took a deep breath. I reminded myself this was an opportunity. I could help my child improve his conflict management skills. I walked over to Trevor and asked him to look into the face of the crying friend. I asked him to notice the sand covering his friend's face and imagine the burning sensation in his friend's eyes. As I worked on helping the friend remove the sand, I asked Trevor how he would feel if the friend had thrown sand into his face. We discussed the frustration Trevor felt that led to the incident and alternative options for handling his emotions. I continued matter-of-factly, "Trevor you are a wonderful person. Your behavior was inappropriate. It hurt your friend and could have damaged his eyes. You are capable of better decisions." Trevor apologized to his friend. His friend apologized for stealing the bucket. They resumed playing. As I returned to where the friend's mom was sitting, I noticed softness had returned to her face too.

Calmly help your child process the situation. Emphasize her ability to make positive choices. Reinforce her personal value. Your child will learn to internalize her own self-control. This will provide long-term safety and a sense of accomplishment.

Let's say siblings are fighting. Consider saying, "It is understandable you are frustrated and angry that your brother changed the channel in the middle of a show. Hitting him is an unacceptable response."

Depending on the situation, you may want to proceed with asking both siblings to stop and consider other options. Do they need space to calm down before further discussion? Other times it may be appropriate to offer an option: "You may both agree on a channel, or all electronics will be turned off for the night." Or: "While I understand you do not feel well, I expect you to treat your brother with respect or place yourself in your room until you feel better and can be respectful."

## Simple but not Always Easy

When your child misbehaves, your objectivity can create a teachable moment instead of escalating events. Take a few deep breaths, count to ten, or do whatever works for you to regain or maintain your composure. Your self-restraint is essential, both as a role model and for your ability to maintain your authority. For example:

> Every day it was the same conflict—Jacob refused to get dressed. The crying, the screaming, the fits were taking their toll on us all. We tried cajoling, bargaining, demanding— nothing seemed to work. Jacob was late to preschool, and my partner and I were both late to work and at each other's throats. Had it only been three days? It felt like a hundred. We were all completely frazzled. Overnight, a

smooth routine had become a major battle. The parenting program in my head said I needed to get a handle on my son and control him. But even at two years of age, I knew I had limited control. Sure I was stronger than him. I could force the clothes on him and drag him out the door, but at what price to my sanity and our relationship? I decided to step back and slow down. It occurred to me that Jacob's fits were not about us. They were about his need to have some control over his own life. After his bath and pj's, Jacob and I stood before his closet. We talked about the weather and activities for the next day. I allowed him to choose his next day's outfit from a selection of clothes. I laid them out. The next morning he dressed without complaint. Oh the relief!

It is that simple. Sometimes it is not so easy, but it is that simple. Figure out the real concern or the unmet desire. Come up with a solution that meets both of your needs. Move out of your need to control. Resolution will come more quickly and with better results when you step into respect, compassion, and a willingness to compromise.

## Ouch!

Chances are fairly good that at some point you will hear the words: "I hate you!" or "You are so mean!" Acknowledge internally it hurts—*a lot*—but realize these outbursts are normal. Even more importantly, understand that sometimes your child is acting out because she feels safe with you. Her pain is over something else, like being left out of a group, an embarrassment in front of friends, or feeling inadequate in a school subject. You are the safe place to let off steam. Respond to her, but not to what she is saying. Show her compassion in the midst of her pain. While you may not approve of or appreciate her current behavior, reinforce that you still love her.

## Whose Issue Is It?

Take the pressure off yourself to always offer an immediate consequence. Sometimes a delay allows you time to clearly determine what you want to accomplish and how to best relay the message. It also provides an opportunity to analyze whether you are reacting to something going on within yourself that has little or nothing to do with your child: disappointment with a coworker, frustration over the traffic, sheer exhaustion, responsibility overload, feeling inadequate, the desire to control, or concern over a friend or finances.

Your child's acting out may be in response to the tension and strain you are exhibiting. Your emotions can create confusion and anxiety within your child. Her ability to recognize your stress as separate from herself is a skill that takes time and self-awareness to develop. You can help your child by acknowledging your feelings. Be the adult. Assure her she is not responsible for your emotions or for making you feel better. Even if you are allowing your child's behavior to add to your stress, you are still responsible for your thoughts, emotions, and behaviors. If necessary, provide yourself a time-out. Remember all emotions are okay. They are insights into your thoughts and needs. How you handle your emotions impacts your child.

## Residual Attitude

Frequently check in with yourself. Is your behavior optimizing the odds of successfully creating the relationship you want to have with your child? An illustration:

En route to soccer practice, Joshua mouthed off to me in front of his friend. It was the second time in a week. The first time I ignored his behavior. I knew he had been under a lot of stress and was overly tired. This time as he said, "You are making us late again. You're driving sucks!" I knew I had to address the behavior. I felt belittled and appalled. I wanted to return a sarcastic remark or tell him he was grounded. Instead, after we arrived at the field, I instructed his friend to join practice and let the coach know Joshua would be there in a moment. Once we were alone, with a sincere desire for understanding, I asked my son, "Joshua, do I show you respect?"

He said, "Yes."

Unemotionally, I continued, "I felt disrespected by your earlier comment. I expect you to show me respect. If at any time I fail to show you respect, please come to me in private and let me know."

Joshua responded, "You are too sensitive. It was only a joke."

I replied calmly, "I felt disrespected. I show you respect, and I deserve and expect the same from you."

Joshua rolled his eyes and complained that
he was late to his practice.
Matter-of-factly, I stated, "Joshua, I deserve
your respect."
He sighed. I encouraged him to have a good
practice.

During a confrontation, your child will likely have some
residual attitude. Avoid responding to it. Make your point and
let the rest go. Allow time for the information to sink in. You
deserve respect. Model the behavior. Realize it may take several
times or situations for your child to fully understand where the
line is crossed. Trust your child will learn the concept.

## Facing the Fury

Determine what boundaries you deem essential. Why
are these important to you? Your child will have more of an
inclination to comply if you keep the number of rules to a
minimum and you articulate your reasons clearly. For all the
rest, use a variety of tools, think outside the box, give options,
and be okay with reconsidering your decisions as you gain
information.

If your child proceeds with a behavior outside your
rules, do you have any meaningful consequences? Is the
issue worth having to impose the consequence? Generally
speaking, consequences usually impact the parent as much as
the child. Taking away car privileges may mean you have the
inconvenience of chauffeuring. And her cruel words or cold
shoulder attitude can be a real heartache. Regardless, there are
many times you need to stand up to and for your child. You have

to face her fury and look past her saying she hates you. You have to stay involved, even when you want to turn away. First, to let her know she is valuable. Second, to set boundaries on appropriate behavior. And third, to protect her, whether from the consequences of her immediate actions or the long-term implications of her choices.

## Be Patient, Be Forgiving ... Repeat

Parenting involves continuous trial and error and tremendous patience. As your child matures and explores, you must adapt and change your parenting tools. When she is two and throwing a tantrum because she wants candy at the grocery store, you may choose to pick her up and leave the store. When she is twelve and she refuses to get in the car, picking her up is a less viable solution. If you create alternative responses when she is two, then you will have more options in your tool bag when she is twelve.

Analyze what it is you want your child to learn. Is it that she must do what you say and respect authority? Or do you want her to understand that sometimes we don't get what we want and it is okay to feel disappointed, but appropriate behavior is still required.

> Patience is a holy key that will unlock the door to a more fulfilling life. Behind the blessed door of patience are found better parents, powerful teachers, great businessmen, wise masters and a more compassionate world.[4]

—Steve Maraboli

## The Power of a Kind Word

You lay the groundwork for positive behavior by spending quality time with your child. Validate the behaviors you do want. Show interest when she shares a new discovery, and she will be motivated to learn and share again. Catch her doing constructive behaviors: brushing her teeth, sitting patiently, being kind to her brother, telling you about her day. Reinforce those actions with a smile, a hug, a compliment—your focused attention. Explain the purpose of certain behaviors—how manners help us to get along in society or how good grades help with college acceptance. Understanding the usefulness of a particular behavior is much more motivating than responding with, "Because I said so." Remember your child loves you and craves your attention. Focus on finding behaviors to praise, and those needing correcting will diminish.

Climbing Mount Everest demands the guide's alertness to each of their clients and each of the clients respecting the expertise of the guide in conjunction with listening to their own internal voice. Parenting entails a similar balance of personal awareness and objectivity along with tremendous patience. Slow down and make your interactions purposeful and deliberate. Cultivate your child's inner desire to behave. In the difficult moments, move off the stage and into the theater seat. Look beyond your child's persona, immediate phase, or behavior. Accept her. Respond with kindness in spite of the circumstance. Remember that she is more than the immediate moment.

## CHAPTER 4

---

# Tell Me the Truth—Even When It Is Hard to Say and Hear

### *The Value of Truth*

Success of Mount Everest climbers is dependent upon the skills of the porters, guides, and fellow climbers; the accuracy of the weather reports; and the ropes and ladders previously installed. Before reaching the summit, Edmund Hillary jumped a crevasse and landed on a chunk of ice that broke off. He went tumbling downward. Just in time, Sherpa Norgay tightened the rope that bound them together, saving Hillary's life.

Developing trust between you and your child is an essential rope. It is established by telling the truth, expecting the truth, having a willingness to hear the truth, and taking responsibility for the truth. Creating an honest relationship with your child begins with you. It lays the foundation for how your child perceives you, as well as how he interacts with you and with others.

## Actions and Images

Are you honest about who you are? How well do you know yourself? What limits do you put on yourself? Do you recognize your talents, acknowledge your faults, and accept responsibility for your needs? When faced with moral dilemmas, like whether to give money to a homeless person, do you know how you would respond and, more importantly, the reason? Do your actions in daily life reflect what you value? Does your outward image accurately reflect who you are internally?

## Building Blocks of Trust

From the moment your child arrives in this world, the simple act of attending to his needs begins to build trust. These acts develop an unspoken promise that you can be relied upon. This strengthens your child's self-image. It establishes you as someone to respect. As your child grows, you model trust with your actions, your words, and your choices—the sitters you choose, whether you pick him up on time from school, what boundaries you set, whether you acknowledge and apologize for your mistakes, and what he hears you say behind someone's back.

When you return an overage of change paid from the teller, you let him know telling the truth is important, even if no one else knows. If you espouse to care about the larger view of the world and he sees you involved in the community, he witnesses the modeling of integrity. When you establish boundaries on your time, space, and emotions and allow your child to do the same, you let him know you and he are both valuable. You both have the right to be honored. Demonstrate this by permitting time for yourself, knocking before entering, and expressing emotions appropriately.

Trust is also built when you set clear, consistent consequences for inappropriate behavior and follow through on the consequences. Your child learns what to expect and to trust there is some order to life. Just as important is guiding your child in recognizing his mistakes and how to learn from those mistakes. If he spills while attempting to pour juice and you yell at him, he learns to avoid trying new things. However, if you help him clean up and then work with him on how to pour the juice, he learns to trust you and to trust in his own ability to learn. Face and accept your own mistakes or those of your child, whether accidental or through poor choices. It will provide an opportunity to learn and grow.

### A Bigger Canvas Please!

The first lie your child tells is often to cover up an action he knows is wrong or he suspects may bring a negative reaction from you—such as, the crayon drawing on the wall or the roll of toilet paper shredded on the floor. The reason for lies usually stems from fear—the fear of disappointing you, of embarrassment, or of consequences. Criticizing him for making a mistake or for not following directions reinforces his fear. Whenever time and circumstance allow, work on uncovering his motivation instead of immediately responding directly to the lie or even the misbehavior.

Did he run out of drawing paper or become curious about how the crayon color would look on the wall? Did he want a different angle to draw from or need a bigger canvas? Your expression of curiosity does not mean you condone drawing on the wall. It simply means you seek to understand and help him process the reason for his decision. Then you can lead the discussion to more appropriate ways to meet both his needs and your needs. For example, buy more paper, attach several sheets to the wall, or provide a specific wall (maybe in the basement) where crayon is allowed. By guiding him to uncover his own motives and process alternative choices, you help remove the need for lying. You empower him to be honest about his needs and actions. You instill in him the importance of integrity—of speaking and living the truth.

## The Heavy Lifting

Creating an atmosphere for honesty requires an ongoing commitment to the relationship. It involves being open-minded and open-hearted. Emphasize that you are always on his side. You may not always like his behavior, but you always love him. Encourage him to be honest with himself and with you. Verbalize to him that you are open and willing to hear the truth. Of course, this means having enough courage on your part to hear the truth! If your three-year-old tells you he accidentally cracked the computer screen when he threw a screwdriver, it can be more than a little aggravating. Having your nine-year-old tell you he stole from the neighbor or your fifteen-year-old tell you she is having sex or doing drugs takes facing the truth to a whole new level. Your own inadequacies raise their ugly head: a fear of failure, the judgment from your friends, or a sense of powerlessness to protect your child. Your world has shifted. It can feel devastating. Take a few minutes alone to absorb and contemplate the information. Allow your emotions to calm before responding. The most important part in creating a safe environment for telling the truth rests in your reaction. These are the moments when you are called upon to handle the heavy lifting of parenting. Certainly you want to express the deep disappointment you may feel in your child's choices. Recognize, though, the behavior of your child is separate from your child as a person. Identify what happened and why it happened and then determine the best action going forward. Has the event itself been enough of a learning experience? Does he understand the effect his behavior has had on the others involved? Is restitution, an apology, or service needed to make amends? It is tempting to kick yourself, overreact, or use emotional blackmail—"How could you do this to me?" You may even contemplate walking away from the relationship. Instead, face the truth, both about your child's actions and your own, as well as whatever led to the situation. It will take incredible courage. The good news is it can result in tremendous growth for you, your child, and your relationship.

In determining the next step, keep the relationship you aspire to have with your child in the forefront. Be honest with yourself about how you feel. Do you want to punish or control him? Are you overwrought with embarrassment? Take a moment to reexamine your values. Analyze the reasons you believe the behavior was inappropriate. Determine how to best communicate this to your child. For example:

> Let's say you are at a restaurant, and your child begins to bend and damage the forks. You may be stunned and feel appalled or ashamed. Take a deep breath! Ask yourself: What is the specific reason you are upset? Are you afraid of judgment from others? Are you concerned you may have

to incur the cost of replacing the silverware? Are you confused as to why your child thinks it is okay to destroy someone else's property, making you wonder about your parenting skills? Next, ask yourself what message you want to relay to your child—no one saw, so we can hide the forks; this is inexpensive silverware, so it doesn't matter; or the property of others is not ours to damage, period, and we owe restitution. Remember your child is watching and learning. Calmly, with as much curiosity as you can muster, ask your child his reasoning for bending the forks. Ask him if he is aware the silverware belongs to the restaurant. Does he realize damaging other people's property is called vandalism? It is against the law. How would he feel if someone damaged *his* personal belongings? Once you have a clear understanding of the reasons *behind* your emotions and your child's thought process leading to his behavior, you will be in a better position to act.

Explaining the reason a behavior is inappropriate is often sufficient to prevent future events. You help your child develop empathy by also clarifying how others have been impacted by his behavior. Explain how his behaviors affect his life. Reinforce your belief in him and in his ability to make more appropriate choices. If your child makes a behavior choice he knew was wrong, clearly state your feelings, the behavior you expect, and the consequences of unacceptable actions. Your commitment to face the complete truth of the situation is crucial. It will determine your ability to see yourself and your child through the challenge.

## Rocks in the Backpack

Lies are fairly common in our society. Whether it is the little white lie to protect someone's feelings or the omission of information to mislead a person, it is still a lie. Ultimately, lies lead to mistrust. One of the challenges is that deception often complicates and obscures the original issue or need. Deception gains weight like putting rocks in a backpack. No matter how much you may think a little white lie will protect your child, it does just the opposite. It causes hard feelings, erodes trust, and deteriorates the relationship.

People will say they would prefer to hear the truth—for someone to tell them if they have a smudge on their face. Yet frequently they fail to muster the courage to tell someone else the same thing. The prevalence of promoting these omissions or little white lies begins early. It is demonstrated in our culture with Santa and the Tooth Fairy. But attempt to be the mom or dad who prefers not to promote such time-honored myths, and the neighborhood wrath may come upon thee. While these cultural lies may be out of your control, you do have complete control over the trust you establish with your child.

## Quagmires

What importance do you place on maintaining others' secrets? Is a confidence always sacred? Is ratting out a person never acceptable? Is it your duty to report the wrong doing of another? Does it depend on the circumstances or whether there is potential harm to someone? Based on where you stand on this issue, your child may find himself in conflict with how to honor your expectation and how to maintain the confidence of a friend. If you teach him to analyze his motive and determine the potential consequences of those decisions, he can begin to work his way through the quagmire. It is important for him to understand where you stand. It is also important for you to respect his decisions.

> The only thing necessary for the triumph of evil
> is for good men to do nothing.

> —Edmund Burke

## Bank Deposits

Inevitably there will be a time when your actions create a breach of trust between you and your child. Perhaps your child will hear you tell a lie to a friend or catch you protecting him with a little fib. It can be tempting to justify your actions. Certainly looking at your intent and decision making is helpful. It will give you a better understanding of what happened and how to prevent repetition in the future. Ultimately, you need to rebuild the trust. You do this by accepting responsibility, expressing sincere remorse, and stating expectations of yourself going forward. Most importantly you follow through on your commitment. For instance:

> I misinformed my daughter while we were shopping. I needed to rectify the situation. "I thought telling you the skirt looked cute would prevent you from getting upset at me and would

help you to feel better about yourself. What I
failed to understand is you are mature enough
to hear the truth and realize the skirt does not
define your beauty. You are a beautiful, fantastic
person, and I love you. I apologize for lying
and for underestimating your maturity. I hope
you will forgive me. I commit to trusting you
and being honest with you in the future." Then
follow through on the commitment!

When you read the example, did it feel over the top? Even
minor offenses are significant given your power as the parent
and the value you place on the relationship with your child.
Consider this: By breaching the trust, you have metaphorically
withdrawn a hundred dollars from your child's bank account
without her permission. Your child feels violated. Redepositing
the hundred dollars may seem fair and would repair the
infraction. Depositing an extra fifty provides emotional
restitution. An apology can merely correct the error, or it can
go further and also help to deepen the trust going forward.

## The Best Safety Net

Building trust with your child means he will be more
likely to ask for your guidance and advice. He will trust you
as a sounding board when he needs to vent. This may require
hearing things you would prefer to avoid hearing or dealing
with uncomfortable issues. Will you actually be able to handle
your child's raw honesty? Consider the following:

My teenage daughter and her boyfriend had been going out for several months. She informed me they were planning to have sex. She wanted to start taking the pill. Internally I felt panicked, total disbelief. I wanted to scream, "Noooo," and lock her in her room! Instead, I took a deep breath, and we talked. I asked questions: What did having sex mean to her? What did she think it would mean to the relationship? Did she feel any pressure from her boyfriend or her peers? Had she promised her boyfriend she would have sex? Was her perception that all teenagers were already having sex? Did she feel prepared? How did she think she would feel if the relationship ended?

We talked about sexual desire being normal and healthy and about satisfying the desire herself. I reviewed safe sex practices—protecting herself from pregnancy, as well as sexually transmitted diseases. We discussed the emotional attachment of intercourse, the societal change from marrying when you're thirteen to waiting until you're closer to thirty, and the benefits of sex within a marriage. And then I told her what I thought: this is a very grown-up decision with potentially serious consequences; I would preferable she wait until she was older; I hoped she would reconsider. I thanked her for talking with me. I agreed to take her to see the doctor. I reinforced that I truly felt her best interest would be to delay such an important decision but I stressed I would honor her decision.

When your child finds acceptance in your willingness to discuss difficult topics, you have an opportunity to impart your wisdom and provide information. It may or may not influence the final decision. Staying calm and detached is tough business! Courage is required. Reach deep into your being and find gratitude in your child's sharing. Remember that trust is one of the best safety nets you can provide your child.

For climbers, it can be difficult to hear the weather is not cooperating or the oxygen supply has run low, but failure to acknowledge these truths can mean death. So too, failure to nurture trust with your child causes the oxygen in your relationship to weaken. Your connection diminishes and frays. Have the determination to value truth and the fortitude to teach your child the same.

CHAPTER 5

# Feeling Special ... Just Like Everyone Else

## *A Soul to Soul Connection*

Mount Everest summiteer Susan Harper Todd compared her Sherpa, Ang Nuru, to a life coach. She noted that he was:

> Someone ... who understands and respects the mountain, who knows the mountain, who lives and breathes it ... He not only showed me the way but, more importantly, he gave me the belief and encouragement that I did have the necessary qualities to do what I really wanted to do, to be able to fulfill my dream ... I was still doing the hard work, putting one foot in front of the other, climbing up rock and ice. Yes, he would occasionally unclip my harness from one rope and attach it on to another, but it was his very presence that was reassuring ... He was encouraging, supportive. He was giving me

permission to realize my dream without taking my power away. He knew I could do it, he saw the qualities in me, he understood the mountain, the task I had set myself and he knew there was no doubt I would reach the summit.[5]

As a parent, you want your child to reach the summit of her dreams. You want her to feel completely and totally loved, for her to recognize that her value is based on the fact that she exists—period. You want your child to know she has boundless potential. She can accomplish anything her heart desires. Her life can make a difference. And whatever obstacles she encounters in life, she can overcome. You want a shield to surround and protect her from all harm and for her to have an internal confidence guiding her every decision. At the same time, you want your child to be humble as she admires the great feats of others, compassionate when she sees others struggle, and fearless when she confronts monumental challenges.

How can you build your child's confidence for overcoming obstacles and instill courage to face her fears while developing humility in dealing with others? What can you do to make your child feel the depth of your love and awe? In a 2000 interview with Oprah Winfrey, Toni Morrison shared the following:

When your child enters the room, does your face light up? When my children used to walk in the room, when they were little, I looked at them to see if they had buckled their trousers or if their hair was combed or if their socks were up. You think your affection and your deep love is on display because you're caring for them. It's not. When they see you, they see the critical face. But if you let your face speak what's in your heart ... because when they walked in the room, I was glad to see them. It's just as small as that, you see.

## Confidence Building

Helping your child feel valued is as simple as pausing and recognizing her presence with reverence—a smile. It helps her to feel like she is really seen, really heard and that she really matters. Light up when your child enters the room. Allow her to see the reflection of her importance in your eyes. Let her know the joy you feel in spending time with her. Show her respect through using good eye contact, keeping a civil tone in conversation, and avoiding interruptions during your interactions, such as answering your phone. Emphasize the importance of your child respecting herself. Teach her ways to demonstrate self-respect: maintaining good hygiene, using good posture, and speaking up for herself. Allow opportunities for your child to explore and follow her dreams. Empower her by offering support and reassurance. Confirm to your child she has the necessary qualities to succeed. Encourage your child to complete a task even when it feels unachievable. Each of these promotes your child's confidence and personal worth.

## Exploring Together

When your child indicates a passion, even if you doubt the validity of her ability, keep an open mind. If she is interested in theater, set up a stage area and give her old clothes to dress up in. Read stories or plays she can then perform. If your child is interested in basketball, take her to a local game, whether it is high school or professional. Together, research skills to improve her game. Have fun practicing together or at least observe her practicing. Each time your child explores an activity, she becomes more aware of her own talents and passions. Each time she runs into difficulty accomplishing a goal, she has an opportunity to stretch her abilities and practice perseverance. This deepens your child's courage and her sense of confidence.

While encouraging your child's talents is important, it is also important to keep her grounded and well-rounded. Few children grow up to be professional athletes or movie stars. Children's athletic and academic abilities develop at different rates. Sometimes they excel in an area while they are young, only to plateau later. One year they are skipping a grade or enjoying the limelight as the best pitcher. A couple of years later their skills have leveled out or an injury ends a promising season. This can be dramatic and demoralizing, especially if they have narrowed their focus on only their strengths. Create opportunities for your child to have new experiences and to continually develop a variety of skills.

## A Piece of the Puzzle

Feeling valued also requires a balance of understanding that our deepest value is in our relationships within society. Each piece of a picture puzzle is essential. Its real value, however, is shown through its placement within the whole. Do you know your value, your aptitudes? Do you constantly compare yourself to others, wishing you were someone else? Do you embrace your uniqueness, appreciate the talents of others, and remain open to learning and evolving?

Help your child understand and appreciate her unique value. Comparing herself to others can make her vain or bitter. Embracing the importance of her strengths reduces self-judgment and the fear of judgment from others. It provides courage for standing up to bullies. It inspires her to share her talents with others and to become a role model for others to emulate. It allows her life to shine.

## Agree to Disagree

Being seen as different can feel very uncomfortable, especially when there is peer pressure to conform and to fit in. How comfortable are you when other people question your viewpoint or disagree with your opinion? Do you avoid confrontation, go on the attack, or listen with curiosity to the opposing opinion? Consider the following:

> I called out to Abbey, who had stepped out of the room. I wanted her to know her favorite song was playing. She ran back into the room, listened for a moment, and then said, "Oh, that's a stupid song."
>
> Last week it had been her favorite. I was confused. "Abbey," I said, "I thought that was your favorite song. What changed your mind?"
>
> She responded, "Kylie said it was stupid, and I agree."
>
> I asked whether she thought the words were still inspiring.

She did, but added, "It is still stupid."

Now my curiosity was up, as well as my concern over how Abbey came to her decision. "Is Kylie a new friend?" I asked casually.

"Yes," Abbey said. "She just moved here, and she is really popular!"

I expressed interest in knowing more about the new friend. General information at first, but when Abbey mentioned Kylie was really bossy, I decided the conversation needed to go further. "I am glad everyone is helping Kylie to feel welcome. It sounds like she is very outgoing. Do you enjoy being around her?" I asked.

"Everyone likes her!" said my daughter in exasperation.

I continued, "That is wonderful. It feels good to be liked. It is okay to ask yourself if Kylie is someone *you* enjoy being around, if you respect her. It is great to have new friends. It is important to be kind to all people. It is also okay to discern whether you respect this person enough to alter your viewpoint on a song or anything else. And it is okay to like something even if your friend disagrees. A real friend allows you the right to honor your own opinion."

If your child believes her viewpoint only has value when others agree with her, she will constantly mold herself to other people's opinions. Or she will only surround herself with people who agree with her. Teach your child to respect the views of others while being true to her own values and ideals. Encourage her to understand how she came to her opinion. Reinforce that it is okay if her viewpoint is different from yours or someone else's. Remind your child her viewpoint is important, even when different. Emphasize the value of remaining open to alternative perspectives—the ability to learn something new or have a deeper understanding. Encourage your child to value herself while also honoring the right of others to have differing opinions.

## Thirty-One Flavors Enrich Life!

It is often said variety is the spice of life. A box of twelve crayons is fun, but a box of one hundred twenty makes drawing even more interesting! Chocolate, vanilla, and strawberry ice creams are all delicious, but what fun to experience thirty-one or more flavors! It is the very variety of people, perspectives, and experiences that enrich life. Encourage your child to embrace the variety life offers and accept her personal uniqueness. At the same time, help her realize society is constantly calling her to conform. Certainly, conforming to some societal rules and manners is important. They help us get along. And whether we like it or not, we are judged by others if we wear a T-shirt, sneakers, and jeans to a formal affair or belch loudly at a dinner party. Helping your child understand the rules of society paves an easier road for her. Your child may rebel, on some level, to some of the societal rules. It is best, however, for her to know the rules and make a conscious decision to be a nonconformist than to be berated for a lack of understanding.

Comprehending the value of manners, while also having respect for herself and others, helps your child develop empathy. She learns that infringing on others' rights is unacceptable, like kicking the airplane seat in front of her, grabbing a toy from someone's hand, or belittling another. Modeling respect for others reinforces the importance of manners, like wiping off the workout equipment for the next person, placing the grocery cart in the return cart holder, or holding the door open for someone whose hands are full. As you encourage your child to recognize and develop her individuality, reinforce the importance of respecting the rights of others. Inspire her to understand she is equal to but not more deserving than anyone else.

## The Birthday Wish List

If you have more than one child, helping them each feel valued is an additional balancing act. Work toward spending special time alone with each one. Share their individual interests—building a train set, riding bikes, or collecting coins. Help them understand how their individuality enhances the family and society; one may be very outgoing and therefore great at getting everyone excited about participation, while the other child may be shyer, and her tenderness helps others feel more at ease. Acknowledge and support their distinct strengths. Encourage each child to express themselves and pursue their individual interests. Help them understand that just as their birthday wish lists will be different from one another, so too are their gifts. The support and the praise they receive from you may be different based on their personal needs. Also allow your children time alone together to connect and enjoy one another. Their empathy and bond will deepen as they learn to share, negotiate differences, respect one another's feelings, and be happy for each other.

## Setting the Mood

Dinnertime provides an awesome opportunity. Occasionally make your child's favorite meal. Develop rituals for communicating with one another. Take turns saying a blessing or expressing what you are grateful for that day. Reflect on the many people involved in bringing food to your table: growers, pickers, truckers, packers, and store handlers. Have each person share the funniest event of the day, a new fact or word they learned, or something about an experience. Encourage an open discussion on a specified topic, allowing each person to have the floor. When interruptions occur, discuss appropriate listening skills. If needed, consider using a talking stick to establish turns. Reinforce the great value in respecting one another's opinions in sharing, as well as in listening and feeling heard.

Evening rituals also offer opportunities. Prior to bedtime, involve your child in the routine of cleaning up both her own space and the shared space—such as, putting toys away and taking dirty dishes to the dishwasher. Discuss the next day's schedule, including school, meetings, doctor appointments, volleyball, tutoring, or the dinner menu. Set expectations for each person's responsibilities: "I will get dinner organized, and I need you to pack your lunch." Review the time she needs to be up and ready to leave, weather or special events that may affect her clothing choices, or equipment needed for a particular activity. Discuss upcoming situations that may have emotional triggers—for example, "I have a late meeting with my department. I plan to pick you up on time. If I am a few minutes late, I hope you will understand," or, "You've spent a lot of time preparing for your presentation tomorrow. Let's see it going great! Besides holding that vision, what else can I do to support you?"

At bedtime, create a relaxed atmosphere. Encourage your child to share something for which she is grateful. Read a book together. Discuss a shared show or movie. Reflect on positive behavior you observed from her, especially a new or developing behavior: "I enjoyed hearing about your book report; thank you for sharing," or, "I really appreciated your taking extra time to help Grandma."

## The Common Bond

As your child approaches the teen years, her desire to fit in may be more consuming. If she wears glasses, has a lisp, or is overly large or small for her age, she may not enjoy being seen as different. Help her understand it is natural to feel awkward when her body is changing and to feel uncomfortable in new settings or when making new friends. Acknowledge it is common to feel embarrassed when you make a mistake, feel rejected if not asked to a party, or feel humiliated when being ridiculed. Give her permission, in addition to feeling excited, to feel nervous when she first learns to drive or to feel apprehensive when preparing to leave home for camp or college. Share with her that even adults want to know what the dress code is for a social event so they will fit in with the crowd. Explain most everyone has experienced feelings of awkwardness, of not fitting in, and of feeling alone. And, oddly enough, the feeling of being different is so common that it bonds us together.

## Stepping Stones

Life occasionally feels unfair. Your child will benefit from understanding this reality sooner rather than later. At different times and to varying degrees your child is going to experience disappointment and feelings of inadequacies. Teach her to understand that everyone has challenges. Encourage your child to see challenges as opportunities, as stepping stones on the path to success. Explain that setbacks and difficulties build resiliency and determination. They ultimately make your child stronger. The blowing wind may seem detrimental to a tree. In most cases, the swaying actually strengthens the tree's roots, helping it to withstand storms.

Whatever challenge your child may encounter, it will most often, though she may not feel that way, just be an inconvenience. In *Uh-Oh: Some Observations from Both Sides of the Refrigerator Door*, Robert Fulghum shares a time he was working at a resort. After being served the same meal every day for a week, he was ready to quit. He began ranting his frustrations to the night auditor, Sigmund Wollman, a survivor of Auschwitz. Wollman replied:

> You know what's wrong with you? It's not wieners and kraut and it's not the boss and it's not the chef and it's not this job ... you don't know the difference between an inconvenience and a problem. If you break your neck, if you have nothing to eat, if your house is on fire— then you got a problem. Everything else is inconvenience. Life is inconvenient ... Learn to separate the inconveniences from the real problems."[6]

51

Whether it is being ostracized in middle school for being a geek, embarrassed over not having the latest cell phone or coolest shoes, or feeling appalled the only job she can find is working cleanup at a fast-food restaurant, give your child a reality check. Remind her that it is a blessing to have intelligence, a phone, or shoes of any kind and that all jobs are an opportunity and a responsibility.

Explain to your child that attitude is the most important factor in overcoming hurdles. A positive attitude creates more productive thoughts and actions. Reinforce the fact that everyone has hurdles, overwhelming moments, and times of feeling alone, left out, or different. In fact, many have far worse problems or multiple issues at one time. Remind her that it is not the obstacle, but her thoughts and response to the challenge that defines her:

> I am not what happened to me, I am what I choose to become.
>
> —Carl Jung

If you encounter someone who displays an obvious challenge—for example, someone in a wheelchair or missing a hand—attempt to engage in conversation with the person regarding his circumstances. If the person is uncomfortable, discuss with your child, in private, what the person may be going through. The challenges he may be experiencing. Humanize the person by reinforcing the ways in which the person is the same as you and your child. Also point out any ways evident the individual is overcoming the disability.

## Praise and Encouragement

Praise in overcoming obstacles provides encouragement. Overpraising for every little milestone can minimize the value of your compliments, it can produce a skewed self-perception, and it can set your child up for failure in the real world. Raise your child to understand her intrinsic value. Admire her uniqueness. At the same time, emphasize the essential components of responsibility, respect, and excellence.

Encourage your child to develop her identity through personal growth instead of societal labels. In conjunction, help her understand that she has a connection to all the other pieces of the puzzle on this planet. Remind her that she has the right to pursue happiness. As she uses her talents for the greater good, she will become happier. Encourage her to show kindness to those around her, provide assistance to those in need, bring joy by creating a beautiful painting or exhibiting athletic talent, or develop an invention to improve the lives of others. By using her abilities, she has the opportunity to add value. The more she understands and expresses her individual talent, the more joy she will experience.

Give your child a fine reputation to live up to. Expect the best from her. Give her praise and honest appreciation. Encourage her to maintain hope and optimism. Let her know she is enough just because she exists. Remind her often that you believe in her, you are proud of her, and you love her.

Sherpas support, coach, and reassure their Mount Everest clients in order to advance a successful summit. As a parent, you can give your child permission to succeed. Light up when she enters the room. Share important moments and conversations. Demonstrate and treat your child with respect. She will develop a deep sense of belonging, of being loved, and of feeling valued.

Model compassion and acceptance toward yourself and others, and you will encourage your child to develop empathy and humility. Encourage her to explore her talents and interest. As your child reaches for her summit goals, your overall belief in her will allow her to weather disappointments, overcome obstacles, and keep a healthy perspective on challenges.

CHAPTER 6

# Greatest Strength ... Greatest Weakness

## *The Real Value of a Trait*

On his third expedition, David Sharp finally reached the summit of Mount Everest. On his descent, he became distressed and sat under a rock overhang just to the side of the trail. As David sat in the death zone, some forty climbers passed him by on their ascent and again, hours later, on their descent. Sir Edmund Hillary was highly critical of those climbers' decision to make summiting a priority over saving a fellow climbers life.

> ... it doesn't impress me at all that they leave someone lying under a rock to die. I think that their priority was to get to the top and the welfare ... of a member of an expedition was very secondary ... I don't think it matters a damn if he was a member of another party. He was a human being. We would regard it as our duty to get him back to safety.[7]

During the same month and year, a similar situation played itself out. Lincoln Hall successfully summited, but on his descent, he became sickened and confused from altitude sickness. Sherpas attempted to rescue him. As night fell, they determined he was beyond help and their own lives were at risk. They descended and reported him as dead. The next day, Hall was found alive by four ascending climbers. They spent hours giving him oxygen and working to warm his body as they waited for rescuers. All four climbers knew they had given up their own ascent in order to save Hall's life:

> The summit is still there and we can go back.
> Lincoln only has one life.[8]

—Dan Mazur

Mount Everest climbers require single-minded resolve to reach the summit. Is the same determination a weakness if another's life is at risk?

Do certain traits serve you well and yet, on occasion, become detrimental? Have you ever noticed how striving for high standards sometimes turns you into a slave of unrealistic expectations? Does your decisiveness increase your productivity but at times cause you to miss important perspectives? Is your enthusiasm motivating to others yet at times perceived as coming on too strong?

## Is This a Good Thing or a Bad Thing?

Your child's natural tendencies and abilities may function as an asset or a hindrance depending on the circumstances.

How can you help your child maximize his talents while minimizing the challenges? It is through the process of helping him understand, develop, *and* expand his attributes.

Evaluate what behaviors you admire and why. Are these the behaviors your parents encouraged? Are these ones you wish to inspire in your child? Are your child's qualities a mirror of your own? If you see the trait as valuable—for instance, being analytical equals spending time reading or learning—you may praise and encourage these activities. On the other hand, you may consider analytical behavior to be a detriment, as being overly cautious or rigid. If you are amiable, you may value that attribute. You may appreciate your child's cooperative, agreeable attitude. Does the same mannerism make you or your child uncomfortable with confrontation or easily influenced by others?

Qualities you dislike or find difficult to accept in yourself or in your child may cause a great amount of friction in your relationship. If you are a driven person but your child prefers quiet, alone time, you may find his behavior concerning. Perhaps you fear he will be left out of activities or fail to excel. Proceed with caution in regards to pushing him hard to socialize or participate in activities in which you think he needs to have an interest. Inadvertently, you may teach him to loath his own qualities. Instead, respect his contemplative tendency. Help him learn the benefits and appropriate uses for his traits. Recognize that your child's raw ability can be an excellent asset in the right scenario or field. Honor his unique abilities.

If your child has exaggerated traits or physical challenges, it may feel devastating and frustrating. Society tends to value certain traits and physical features over others. A child who is outside the norm may be labeled or discarded as less valuable. Reflect on the following:

Temple Grandin was labeled "unique." She was diagnosed as autistic and branded as brain damaged due to her hypersensitivity, anxiety, and a lack of emotional connection. Instead of having her institutionalized, as the doctor recommended, her mother pushed for her daughter's education. Temple gradually learned to modify and control some of her fixations. This allowed her uncanny power of observation to emerge. Temple came to realize her "weaknesses" were an asset. She thought in highly detailed pictures. She understood the feeling of being threatened by everything in her surroundings, as well as feeling dismissed and feared. These qualities allowed her the distinctive ability to understand how cattle experience details the average person seldom notices, like a puddle or shadows. Her exceptional perspectives revolutionized the practices for humane handling of livestock. Temple Grandin became a doctor of animal science, a professor at Colorado State University, an advocate for autism, a consultant to the livestock industry, one of the design leaders of livestock handling facilities, and named as one of *Time* magazine's 100 Most Influential People in the world.

Advocate for and believe in your child's worth. Your child may develop an important technique or solution, like Dr. Grandin. Or become an inspiration, like Jim Abbott, who, though born with only one hand, became a successful major league baseball pitcher.

## What's in a Word?

Consider the semantics of traits. Some, like obstinate or distractible, tend to conjure up negative feelings. When obstinate is instead labeled as determined, or distractible as curious, our attitude tends to shift. Likewise, some traits shine more brightly in the right situation. If your son always has an argument against every rule in the house, you may consider him stubborn. Might this be an outstanding quality for an attorney or debate team captain? Your daydreaming daughter may be spending time observing the world and imagining it in a different way, a talent of some great writers and scientists. An average athlete usually lacks the strength or talent of a pro athlete. He may be more successful in an Ironman competition, where endurance is the key.

## Star Gazing

In addition to accepting and appreciating your child's attributes, look to inspire complementary traits: "You have really mastered how to be straightforward when expressing your opinion. You may also want to develop tactful ways of expressing your opinion for sensitive situations." Or, "Your playfulness brings a lot of joy to people. When we go to the library, you may want to practice a more reserved behavior to show respect for those who are reading." If your child is a perfectionist, he may keep his room clean and organized. He may also want to develop tolerance for spontaneity. Or if your child is laid back, he may be enjoyable to hang out with. He may also benefit from enhancing his ability to follow through on responsibilities like completing chores. And while being obedient is a positive trait in some settings, it is also important in other situations for your child to know how to stand up for himself.

As your child understands and appreciates his natural tendencies, he will be more willing to embrace additional qualities. Understandably, he will seek out activities and individuals that play to his strengths. His assets bring him comfort. His weaknesses, though, will offer opportunities for personal growth. Learning a new trait takes time and repetition. It will require perseverance. Help him to practice a range of roles and develop ease in a variety of settings.

Let's say your child is very outgoing. He may have lots of friends and be invited to many parties. If he also develops the ability to sit quietly and listen, he increases his opportunities to learn from others, broadening his knowledge. Encourage this development by creating occasions for quiet moments— observe the stars, read a story together, explore the woods, watch a sunset, or take turns asking each other questions about favorite things.

If your child is quiet and reserved, he may have a strong ability to concentrate and examine data. If he also learns to speak up for himself and ask for help, he increases his comfort level in social settings. He learns to feel more assertive in expressing his opinions. Encourage social interactions— rehearse how to discuss and what to say with his teacher or coach and then have him initiate the actual conversation, make the extra effort to include him in the conversation during social interactions, or play charades or other games that encourage spontaneity.

Your child will most likely continue to prefer particular situations and lean toward certain behaviors. However, his expanded comfort zone and abilities will provide a sense of security and self-reliance.

## Skill Building

Good communication skills will benefit your child socially and emotionally. Advise him on the importance of listening with the sincere intent of understanding the other person. Help him appreciate the benefit of expressing his needs and feelings from an attitude of self-responsibility, instead of a position of blame. For social and business interactions in the United States, teach him to have a firm handshake and encourage him to look people in the eye when communicating.

Assist your child in expanding his language of emotions. Model this skill. Give him specifics when expressing your own emotions: "I am disappointed in myself for letting you down by failing to picking you up on time," "I am astonished the dog was able to open the gate," "I feel exasperated that the room remains a mess," "I am thrilled you feel good about your test," or "I am thankful for you in my life." Then instead of telling his friend he is angry, he will be able to say, "I felt embarrassed when I was made fun of at lunch. I would prefer we only joke with one another in private." By expressing exactly how and why he feels a certain way, he has a better chance of working through disagreements with his friend more quickly and with better results.

An additional way to strengthen your child's abilities is to identify his learning styles. Observe what he enjoys doing in his free time and the language he uses when he complains. Help him pinpoint study methods that play to those strengths. If he likes to draw and work puzzles, perhaps he is a visual learner. When studying, encourage him to highlight key words and phrases or to draw graphs. If he is into sports and games or expresses high sensitivity to physical discomfort, he may be a physical learner. Suggest he walk around while memorizing facts. If he has an affinity for music, putting the facts he needs to memorize into song lyrics might prove useful.

## Explore, Explore, Explore

Your child, like most people, may not shine with a special talent right out of the gate. Observe what your child gravitates toward. Offer multiple experiences, so he can discover what he enjoys. If your son never wants to leave the pool, perhaps a swim or dive team may be a fitting activity. A child constantly in motion may be suited for gymnastics or excited about setting up a mini-Olympics in the backyard. Give your child freedom to explore, expand his vision, and grow. Be prepared to recognize strengths as they appear.

If your child is reserved and hesitant to participate in activities, will you require participation? Evaluate your child's reasons for not wanting to participate. Is it fear of failure or social awkwardness? Offer your time as a volunteer to increase his comfort level. Consider an individual sport, such as tennis, or noncompetitive activity, such as a cooking class. Accept your child as he is while also encouraging him to stretch and attempt new things. Reinforce the inherent value of continual growth and development. New activities give him the opportunity to discover new strengths and enhance areas where he may lack confidence. Involvement in school activities, especially in high school, is often associated with higher GPA and fewer high-risk behaviors. Requiring your child to commit to at least one activity, sport, or club a year will benefit him socially and academically.

## Commitments—Where's the Line?

The process of discovering your child's talents and interests offers an opportunity for patience. This is especially true in regards to quitting. If your child signs up for lessons or a team but does not like the activity, do you require him to continue? Take into account the level of effort he has expended. Do two violin lessons seem sufficient to make a decision? The soccer team may be counting on him to honor his commitment. If he is a benchwarmer and not making a visible contribution, does it change his responsibility to the team? Is quitting never an option, or is the attempt sufficient? If forced to continue, will he hesitate to try something new in the future? If he is not required to fulfill the commitment, will he learn to quit every time something seems difficult or uncomfortable? As a parent, you need to continually weigh the long-term benefit and responsibility with the short-term challenge.

While offering your child a variety of opportunities and activities to explore, also consider the balance of the family's finances, time, and needs. If your child plays soccer and baseball, takes karate and piano lessons while additionally being involved in Scouts, the schedule may become overwhelming. Contemplate the benefits from each activity. Maybe you want him to choose one sport because he is athletic. Perhaps stay involved in Scouts to further his citizenship and leadership skills. Or, instead continue with piano lessons because of its intrinsic worth. Review your finances and schedule. Define your values and your goals. Communicate them to your child. Listen to his point of view, his needs, and his interest. Work toward honoring his wishes and your boundaries.

## A Clearer Vision

Michelangelo, when asked how he created his famous statue of David, said he merely removed the unnecessary stone to reveal David. Instead of viewing your child as clay to be sculpted, consider your child was born with traits and gifts. Your role is to help him remove the rough edges and become the best version of himself. Part of the process is in helping him evaluate situations and ask the right questions. If your child indicates he wants to become a graphic designer of video games, work with him to find the necessary skills or classes. Perhaps he will be excited about the photography and music classes. He may be surprised to learn that technical writing classes are also important. Or let's say he expresses an interest in movie making but has a lack of interest in the art of editing. His real enjoyment is in seeing movies. Discuss whether he might prefer becoming a movie critic.

Fear of failure may discourage your child from acting on his dreams, because failure frequently conjures up a derogatory meaning. Let your child know that scientists often find failure to be a useful tool and embrace trial and error as part of the learning curve. Advise him that great discoveries have come from seeming mistakes or after experiencing numerous disappointments—case in point, the discoveries of penicillin, safety glasses, rockets, airplanes, cellophane, Post-it Notes, and Velcro.

> I have not failed 10,000 times. I have successfully found 10,000 ways that will not work.
>
> —Thomas A. Edison+

Inspire your child and yourself to embrace failure as a natural part of education. If he runs up against something that fails to work out, ask him to consider what he learned from the experience. Encourage him to explore what additional effort he needs to expend in order to obtain his goal. If he tries something and discovers it is not what he wants, he will then have an even clearer vision of what he does want.

> Failure is the foundation of success, and the means by which it is achieved.
>
> —Lao Tzu

**Advancing Confidently**

Discuss your child's goals and the skills he needs to hone to ensure he is prepared when opportunities knock. At the same time, realize that at one point or another, your child's goal may seem impractical. It may be helpful for him to know the obstacles he is up against. He also needs to know you believe in him. Trust in his vision for himself. If your child's goals and dreams conflict with your own dreams for him, consider the following quotes from Henry David Thoreau:

> If a man does not keep pace with his companions, perhaps it is because he hears a different drummer. Let him step to the music which he hears, however measured or far away.

> If one advances confidently in the direction of his dreams, and endeavors to live the life which he imaged, he will meet with success unexpected in common hours.

## Personal Excellence

The seeming strength and weakness of many traits is subjective and contextual. Some traits, however, tend to be highly valued across society, in the workplace, and in life in general. Encouraging these qualities in your child will prove beneficial. These traits generally include honesty, integrity, and empathy, being responsible and a good citizen, treating all people with respect and fairness, and pursuing personal excellence.

## Always Listening!

Whatever strengths or weaknesses you perceive your child to have, be careful he is not pigeonholed by you or others as being lazy, uncoordinated, sweet, difficult, etc. Avoid emphasizing a behavior when it shows up in less than desirable ways. It may seem funny when your one-year-old acts silly at dinner, but it will be less welcome by the time he is four. Also, be mindful of what you say about him to others. He is always listening! Continually look for opportunities where his traits can be praised, where his weaknesses can be transformed into strengths, and where he can practice appropriate new behaviors.

Ambition and laser focus are essential in the Mount Everest climber's quest for the summit. Yet, in changing circumstances, these same traits may be viewed as a weakness if he fails to show compassion for his fellow hikers. The value of a trait is often subject to perspective and dependent upon the circumstances. Review the characteristics you deem valuable. Consider the traits your child possesses. Recognize that those qualities may show up as conflict or resolution given the situation. Be open to how his traits can be capitalized on in positive ways. Encourage him to continually stretch and expand his abilities. Assist him in maximizing his current aptitudes by learning to use them in appropriate ways.

CHAPTER 7

# You Make Such Good Decisions ...
# What Were You Thinking?

*Learning What You Do Want*

In 1996 two experienced climbing teams began their trek up Mount Everest. They encountered unexpected delays, ropes not affixed, a struggling client, and a bottleneck of climbers. Instead of reassessing the situation or encouraging a candid team discussion, they maintained their course of action. When the hard-and-fast rule of "summit by 2 p.m. or turn around" came and went, the guides ignored the conventional wisdom to abandon the summit. Their clients had invested time, energy, and money. They did not want to disappoint. When a fierce storm hit, they were taken by surprise. Their commitment to a failing course of action culminated in eight deaths—one of the deadliest days in the mountain's history.

Do you want your child to learn the warning signs of danger? How to heed the caution lights of life? Do you want your child to hone her decision-making skills for creating the life she desires? The process involves your child learning how to assess situations and potential outcomes. It involves her being able to stand up for herself, as well as having the courage to stumble. It requires her willingness to recognize her emotional impulses and selfish motivations.

## The Power of Impulse

Offer your child multiple occasions to practice making decisions. Begin with everyday interactions. Encourage her to pick out the book to read or decide whether to leave her apple whole or cut it into slices. As she becomes more capable, offer increasingly more complex options. Let her suggest where to go for dinner after comparing costs of various places and family members' likes and dislikes or what outfits to purchase after considering school dress codes and quality and comfort of fabric and style. Teach her how to gather facts, weigh options, and brainstorm solutions. She will learn to distill the outcome she truly desires, and she will be better equipped when faced with challenging decisions on her own.

Assist your child in gaining additional insights by looking at other people's choices. Include age-appropriate examples from current movies or headlines. Let's say there is a tragic news report about a child who ran across the street without looking and was killed by a car. Discuss the power of impulse and the resulting consequences. Include the subsequent impact on the parents and sibling who are left behind, as well as on the friends who watched and perhaps even encouraged the behavior. Or if a movie portrays a couple who express passion through violence, discuss the inappropriateness of violence in a loving relationship and which behaviors really do express love. Lead—then listen. You will learn much about your child from her answers. Conversationally add your own opinion. Refrain from taking the position: "I'm the adult, so I'm always right." Show respect for her opinions.

Teachable moments also come in analyzing choices that resulted in less-than-desirable outcomes. For example:

> If your child scores poorly on a test, walk through the various decision points leading to the result. Did she read the chapters, take quality notes, and ask questions on information she did not understand? Did she study over several days? If all of these steps seem consistent with success, help her consider other factors, like whether she is getting enough sleep or whether she may need glasses or a tutor.

Your child wants to succeed. Be caring instead of critical, and you will have her ear. Sometimes your child can feel overwhelmed. She may simply need to know it is okay to ask for help.

## Personal Fallacies

When you make a mistake, do you readily confess, hide the evidence, or look for someone else to blame? Are you able to laugh at yourself and acknowledge your fallacies? If your child makes a mistake, do you immediately think she would never do that? Do you become embarrassed and berate her? Or do you take a deep breath and gather the facts? Check in with yourself. Do you have the courage to let your child make mistakes or to even fail?

Your child's shortcomings can feel like a reflection of your own faults or the shortcomings of your parenting skills. The result can be beating yourself up, burying your head to avoid seeing any faults, or trying to cover them up. These reactions prevent personal growth and positive role modeling. Do you want your child to respect you and see you as an authority figure? First you need to have respect and authority over yourself. Examine your tolerance for acknowledging faults in your child, as well as in yourself.

## The Hidden Gift

How do you handle feedback from others—as an attack or as an opportunity to learn? Are you able to weed out the grain of truth from the emotional sting? Do you view feedback as a threat or a potential gift?

Feedback from others can certainly hurt! It can also offer a hidden gift for self-improvement. Fearing criticism may make your child hesitant to make mistakes, to explore, and to be authentic. Or she may believe, "That's just the way I am, and there's nothing I can do about it," limiting herself instead of considering whether to cultivate a new ability. Alternatively, openness to the potential positive in criticism provides an opportunity to deepen her understanding of herself. She can enhance her skill set and her relationships. Feedback can be like a dreadfully wrapped package with something brilliant inside!

Encourage your child to embrace the potential value of feedback. Teach her how to assess criticism. Reinforce that she is valuable regardless of another person's opinion about her behavior, beliefs, or appearance. Acknowledge her feelings. Then assist your child in unraveling the criticism from her emotional response to the ugly package. Help her decipher what value the person's opinion offers. Encourage her to consider whether any personal change will add value to her life. Let's say her friend tells her she is bossy. Allow your child to recognize she feels hurt, indignant, or ashamed. Then help her consider whether the friend is upset he cannot be the leader all the time. Or whether her own determination to be the leader is jeopardizing the friendship. Analyzing the comment can open a discussion regarding the definition of leadership, how to be a good leader, how to be a good follower, and ways to build or repair the friendship.

Let your child know it is important to love and accept herself regardless of the good opinion of others. At the same time, inspire her to develop a broader awareness of her abilities and limitations by welcoming and evaluating feedback from others.

## The Art of Negotiation

How comfortable are you with your child disagreeing with or questioning your rules and opinions? The process of learning to state her opinion, make the case for what she wants, and disassemble your point of view gives your child a valuable tool. She learns how to articulate her needs, analyze the opposing arguments, and stand up for herself. This progression, when done respectfully and openly instead of defensively, helps her learn the art of negotiation. And it develops her ability to stand up to peer pressure.

## Dark Alley or Dirt Path?

From an early age, your child may make choices you
find questionable. Your son may want to wear a purple hat
to kindergarten every day. Your daughter may refuse to wear
dresses for any occasion. Examine what you value and the
part society and peers may play. If your daughter decides to
date a boy you do not care for, shave her head, get a nose
ring, or drop out of an activity you want her to continue,
seek to truly understand the reasons for her decision. Ask her
the uncomfortable questions with an open, inquiring mind.
Support her in exploring and making a decision with as much
information as possible. Pick your confrontations carefully.
Look to have more discussions than battles.

Examine the innate desire you have to protect your child
and the fear you may be experiencing. Are you concerned
she will be ridiculed or physically or emotionally harmed
in some way? Is the boy she wants to date a violent person
or just a little bit of a slacker? Shaving her head may cause
some embarrassing moments, but hair does grow back. Is
the desire for a nose ring related to social pressures? Does
she understand any risk or health and maintenance issues
involved and the possible social or job market ramifications?
Is she dropping out of an activity because she is burnt out
or because she wants to pursue a different activity? Is she
completely withdrawing from all activities and hanging out
with a new crowd?

Ask *yourself* whether your child is in real danger and needs
protection. Are you simply struggling with her expressing her
independence? Are you experiencing peer pressure from your
friends? Plenty of people will judge you and your decisions.
What is more important—the opinion of your friends or your

relationship with your child? Do you need to convince your child to act a certain way in order to feel valued by fellow parents? Is allowing your child to explore her own identity more important? Contemplate the opinion of those you respect in relationship to the larger view of your parenting goals. Consider whether this is an opportunity to model living your own truth in spite of the peer pressure from your friends. Determine whether the direction your child is pursuing is down a dangerous dark alley or simply a curvy dirt path.

## Pink Hair

As your child stretches her wings and makes increasingly difficult, sometimes life-changing decisions, prompt her to self-examine her motivations and intentions. Let's say she is infatuated with a boy, but her best friend also likes him. Ask her how this might affect the friendship. Does she feel pressure to dress or act a certain way to gain the boy's attention? If these actions are inconsistent with whom she really is or wants to be, will she really be happy? Ask thought-provoking questions to help her examine the situation: What are you hoping will happen? What are the obstacles you face? What are your options? What might be the short-term and long-term consequences? Are you aware that...? And offer some advice: These are some things you may want to consider... Or rephrase the question: If you dye your hair pink and gain the boy but lose both who you are and your best friend, how do you think you will feel?

## Creating Space

Where appropriate, provide space for your child to back down from a decision without losing face. For example:

> Emma asked to decorate her room. At the paint store she excitedly picked out a very deep, dark red color. I wanted to share information with my daughter. "Emma, it is a beautiful color. Before you make a final decision, may I share some information?" She hesitated then said yes. I offered: "It is helpful to envision how you want a room to feel. Deep colors tend to darken rooms, making them feel smaller. Bold colors, especially in reds, create a stimulating atmosphere that can diminish relaxation. Neutral tones tend to encourage restful sleep and may provide more of a highlight for your posters. The choice is yours. I want you to have as much information as possible so you can make an informed decision." Then I was silent to allow time for the information to be absorbed.

As often as possible, ask and receive permission before sharing. Your child will feel less defensive. She will be more receptive to hearing the information. If she says no, say okay and gently back away.

If your child agrees to listen, offer the information nonjudgmentally. Give her the space to process the information. Allow the decision to rest with your child. By holding the power and responsibility for the final outcome, your child will learn to be more open and thoughtful in her choices.

## More than a Puppet

How do you know for sure if your child's decision is good or bad? You may think your child choosing to spend her time and money on an instrument is foolish. You think she needs to focus on becoming a doctor. After all, she is so smart and good in science, and medicine is a more secure, lucrative field. The reality is you have limited control. She is not a puppet on a string. The more you push her into the mold in your head, the greater the chance she will turn away from you or from her own potential. How do you know for sure she is meant to be a doctor? Certainly point out strengths you see. Encourage her to keep the doors of opportunity open. Then believe in your child. Trust she is doing what she needs to do and learning what she needs to learn. You may tell your child you do not understand her decision, but also let her know you have confidence in her. You trust in her ability to make decisions and to choose what will bring her happiness.

## Benefit of Time

As your child grows older and the potential outcome of decisions have heftier consequences, contemplate the level of maturity and responsibility your child has developed. Consider whether encouraging your child to postpone the activity would allow her time to more fully comprehend the possible ramifications of her decisions. For example:

> Your thirteen-year-old daughter buys a revealing halter top. You might say, "Are you aware that wearing a revealing top will result in your being

perceived in a certain way? You will be exposing your bare back. Someone could pull the string or consider it an invitation to touch your back. I prefer you wait until you are more comfortable with your own self and your own body before choosing to wear something so revealing."

Or: If you see your young son make-believe smoking, you might offer, "Choosing to smoke cigarettes is a major decision. Because of the magnitude, legally, socially, and health-wise I hope you choose a smoke-free life. I encourage you to wait until you are at least eighteen before considering such an important decision."

## Helping the Tree Grow

Share with your child that like a drop of water that ripples outward, so do her decisions. Rushing to pour milk may result in a spill. Choosing to speed may result in a ticket or an accident. Showing kindness may produce a new friendship. Stopping at a red light may save her life. And some decisions come with monumental ramifications that can diminish or even eliminate future options, like teenage pregnancy or dropping out of school. Each decision can be like watering a tree to help it grow or cutting off its branches.

Brain development for mature decision making is usually not complete until the mid-twenties. Your child may look grown-up. She may make excellent decisions in some areas of her life. She will, however, make some decisions that will horrify you. Keep communications open. Realize it is normal. Forgive her and yourself.

On more than one occasion in history, a climber took a step too close to an edge, a company made an arrogant decision, or a child chased a ball into the street. When climbing Mount Everest, the team leaders, in order to protect their clients, must be willing to humbly accept that sometimes circumstances prevent them from meeting their clients' expectations. They need to put their egos out of the way, stay attuned to the ever-changing circumstances, and be willing to encourage open, dissenting discussion. As a parent, you have a great deal of influence on your child. But you have limited control over her choices. Provide multiple, ever-increasing opportunities for your child to learn the art of making decisions. Teach her how to assess situations, examine options, and prioritize decisions. Help her understand the value of feedback and of examining her motivations. Embrace the occasional, inevitable agony associated with the learning curve. Allow her the privilege of living with consequences while she has the benefit of your care and wisdom. Believe in her ability. Park your ego and your fears—yes, it is hard, but important! She will hone her decision-making skills. She will take a step closer to internalizing her ability to parent herself and to creating a life that will bring her joy.

CHAPTER 8

# Completely Involved ... Letting Go

## *What You Focus on Expands*

Climbing Mount Everest requires a significant commitment of time—forty to sixty days on average. During that time, the climbers gradually ascend to base camps at higher and higher altitudes. At each camp, the climber spends time acclimating to the ever-diminishing oxygen levels in the atmosphere.

Parenting involves a significant commitment of time. It too requires continuous acclimation to the changing needs of your child. Your newborn baby is unable to care for even his most basic needs of food, clothing, shelter, or safety. He requires full-time care. But within a short period of time, you begin teaching him how to care for himself: holding a cup, changing his clothes, and paying attention to safety issues. Even while he is mastering the basics of self-care, your role begins to evolve. You continue to teach him life skills, but you also become a role model. You become a guide for how to *be* in life.

Who are the role models in your life? Would you choose yourself as a role model? Are you proud of the adult you've become? Do you take responsibility for your choices?

## The Constant Observer

Exhibiting responsibility for yourself and your own actions through self-control and self-discipline improves the chances your child will develop these same skills. Your child absorbs your every word and move like a sponge. Even when you think he is unaware, your actions are filtering into his experience. He is observing whether you gossip, how you treat the sales clerk and your spouse, and whether you offer kindness to strangers.

## Stability and Resiliency

Contemplate what your life and your expectations are communicating to your child. Do you live in rushed chaos? Do you live tied to a routine? Is organization your middle name? Calm, stability, and peace are created with structure, organization, and routine. Does your child have a quiet place for unwinding or working on homework? If you have electronics in every room, is there space for contemplating, reading, or enjoying one another's company? Is there a scheduled snack and playtime prior to working on homework or after? Is there a set bedtime and bedtime routine? When routine is interrupted, are you able to go with the flow and allow for spontaneity and a change in plans? Structure provides stability for your child. Coping with an occasional dose of chaos can add to his resiliency.

## Money, Sex, and More

Do you want your child to feel like a valued part of your family unit? Set up realistic expectations of your child, such as helping with household chores based on his abilities. Offer genuine appreciation for his effort. Reinforce his importance and the importance of his task. When your child is old enough to use an alarm clock, require him to get up and get ready on time. Praise your child's self-discipline, and he will feel further empowered. Help your child understand that school is his job. He is expected to give it his best. He will learn the importance of education, a strong work ethic, and the pride of accomplishment. Your child will begin to understand his role in determining his own future.

How do you handle your finances? Is your child observing careless purchasing or a methodical approach to spending? Do you want your child to understand the value of handling money prudently? Allow him to count out the money for a small item at the checkout, assist him in opening a savings account, and require him to work and save for special purchases. He will gain an appreciation for the value of money. Share with your child the emotional and social benefit of donating. Educate him regarding paying bills on time, impulse buying, credit cards, and the goal of advertisers. Review with your child the purpose and uses of taxes and how to complete tax forms. Take opportunities to explain loans, contracts, and investments. With knowledge, your child will gain confidence and wisdom in handling his future financial decisions.

Do you want your child to live a healthy lifestyle? Spend time together riding bikes, hiking, or swimming. He will begin to associate exercise with fun. If you require your child to get fresh air and exercise regularly, it becomes part of his lifestyle.

If the food in your home and the snacks your child sees you eat are usually healthy, he will have a tendency to eat healthier food. When you place an emphasis on living a healthy lifestyle instead of a body image, your child learns to listen to and take care of his own body in healthier ways.

Are you comfortable discussing your child's sexual development, sex, and birth control? Are you at ease with your own sexual desires and knowledge? Your ability to navigate through this topic can ensure your child has the facts. He is going to obtain information one way or another. Would you rather your child obtain misinformation from peers and the web? Are you counting on the school system to educate your child? If so, ensure familiarity with the curriculum, so you can supplement as needed. Your child's changing body and desires are natural. Help him understand safe sex practices and ensure he understands the significance of his responsibility for preventing pregnancy. Emphasize the importance of having respect for others, even if they fail to have respect for themselves. Highlight the need to honor boundaries—no means no! Your courage to have the uncomfortable discussions will keep your child safer and healthier.

Do you maintain the space in your home? Do you make conscious decisions about the belongings you have and how you care for them? If so, your child will learn the importance of maintaining his belongings. If he has a space of his own he can decorate or where he can display a collection, even if it is a small box or a private journal, he will feel valued. Your child will begin to understand and respect boundaries.

Take your child to an assortment of museums, fairs, sports events, and concerts to help broaden his cultural understanding. Further develop his appreciation for the diversity of humanity by taking him to celebrations of other cultures. The more variety of experiences your child encounters the more globally he will think. Your child will expand his comfort level for diverse settings.

## Snowflakes

There is a natural learning curve when you start a new job or learn a new activity. At first it may seem overwhelming, but as your understanding and skills develop, so does your confidence. Whether it is cooking a meal or completing a home-improvement project, the task becomes easier when it is reduced to smaller steps. The same is true for your child. Simplify the learning process into manageable steps. It will help reduce his frustration and improve his chance of success. An example is the rhyme for learning to tie shoes:

> Bunny ears, bunny ears, playing by a tree.
> Crisscrossed the tree, trying to catch me.
> Bunny ears, bunny ears jumped into the hole,
> Popped out the other side beautiful and bold.

As your child works on learning and mastering each new task, whether it is how to make his bed, build a model, or complete a school project, he gains confidence. He begins to believe in himself and in his ability to succeed.

Give him the chance to pour juice, pick out his own clothes, and make his sandwich. Review how to do the task and/or the possible pitfalls: if you pour slowly, if you hold the jug up really high. Your child will learn there is a process to consider. He will begin to understand complex tasks can be broken down into manageable steps. His step-by-step decisions can affect the outcome. If it takes time for your child to master a task, your confidence in him instills the ability to adapt and persevere.

Each child learns in varying ways. Some are intuitive, while others mimic observations. Some prefer to learn hands-on or need to take things apart. Others are timid and want time to digest the information internally before making an effort. You may notice your child's learning curve is littered with stubbornness, frustration, or even tears. It may be painful to watch. It may take more time than you prefer. But we all have a process. Work with your child. Provide encouragement, time, and space and then believe in him. All snowflakes are formed from a droplet of water and dust/pollen. But as each one descends, the tiniest variations in humidity, wind, and temperature affect the crystals formation. Each one arrives beautiful but unlike the others. Your child too has his own unique process. Trust that he will learn what he needs to learn.

## Outside the Comfort Zone

How comfortable are you with taking on new initiatives, meeting new people, and discussing your views on issues? Parenting constantly urges you to grow out of your comfort zone. When your child plays at a new friend's house, you may feel apprehension. Make the effort to meet the new friend's parents. It will give you the opportunity to determine the validity of any concerns. You will have the chance to build a mutual bond between you and the other parent. And your child will feel valued. Building a relationship with the parents of your child's friends allows you to initiate discussions regarding bike helmets, cell phones, dating, or alcohol. Working toward consistency on these issues with fellow parents helps to promote your child's safety.

Embrace the concept of community. Your child will interact with many different people in the community. Each encounter shapes your child. The less-than-perfect teacher will help prepare him for the not-so-great boss. The teacher he looks up to may be the one with the words of wisdom he needs to hear. The firemen and police officers who protect your home, the neighbor who babysits, and the coach who teaches your child hockey all play an integral part in raising your child. Remember to thank them. Be open to allowing them to share their personal wisdom with your child. Be willing to see your child in the eyes of all children. Your child will learn the value of connecting and caring for others as he watches you do your part to be there for the children and parents in your community.

Involvement with your child through community activities, whether it is a playgroup, religious group, or neighborhood or school event, offers an excellent opportunity for you to observe how your child is developing academically, emotionally, and socially. Attending school conferences signals to the teacher you care, you want to have a cooperative relationship, and you want to head off any problems. Volunteering in the schools with fund-raisers, classroom assistance, PTA, or the school board helps you to keep a pulse on how the school is operating. It reinforces to your child the importance of education and your commitment to being his advocate. One of the great additional benefits from participation in your child's activities is the opportunity for shared fun and communication—a joy to treasure!

## The Great Power of Silence

Being truly involved in your child's life depends on listening and being present in a way that encourages your child to trust you and to seek your support. It requires listening with a degree of detachment, setting aside your initial reaction, and giving your child time to speak fully. There is great power in silence, in just listening. It can often take several minutes before the real issue is uncovered. Give your child the needed time and space. It is natural to want to problem solve, protect, and rescue your child. As often as possible, allow him to work through his issue and hear himself as you listen. At some point, when your child is faced with a decision and you are not there, you will have given him the tools to have the conversation with himself. Contemplate this poignant poem:

> When I ask you to listen to me
> and you start giving advice,
> you have not done what I asked.
> When I ask you to listen to me
> and you begin to tell me why I shouldn't
> feel that way, you are trampling on my
> feelings.
> When I ask you to listen to me
> and you feel you have to do something to
> solve my problem, you have failed me
> strange as that may seem.
> Listen! All I asked was that you listen,
> Not talk or do – just hear me[9]

> —Ralph Roughton, MD

If it is cold outside and your child refuses to wear a coat, do you force the coat on him? If you force the coat on him, have you listened to his needs? Perhaps his temperature gauge is different than yours. Maybe he needs to experience the discomfort of cold in order to understand the warmth of a coat. When your child is getting run down, ask him if he feels the need for additional rest, a healthier snack, or vitamin C or to consider what thoughts might be affecting his body. This encourages him to listen to his body, pay attention to his thoughts, and take responsibility for his health. These experiences teach your child to trust his own instincts.

## Press the Stop Button

It is important for your child to learn respect for authority figures, like coaches, relatives, police, religious leaders, teachers, and doctors. It is also important for him to learn respect for his own inner guidance. There are plenty of stories about authority figures who have taken advantage of a child using their position. These adults prey on children by confusing them. They groom children with kind words and touch that feels good. Gradually, as the child becomes comfortable, the authority figure's behavior crosses over to inappropriate acts. This is very puzzling for a child. The more you learn to listen—really listen—to your child, the more you are able to protect him. Allow him to determine who he is comfortable spending time with or hugging. Pay attention if he seems reluctant to be left alone with a particular person, even if it is someone you respect. If he says he feels unwell or becomes withdrawn around someone, press the *stop* button. Listen to his body language, as well as his words. It may just be a stage your child is going through or a personality conflict with the individual. Regardless, reinforce his right to determine his own personal space and allow him to do so. Your listening empowers his ability to listen to and trust his own instincts. It provides a greater chance he will be able to protect himself from predators.

## Conquering Adversity

Through involvement in your child's life, you may be very in tune with his needs, his likes, and his dislikes. The challenge is to remember that as tuned in as you may be, he has thoughts and desires you may never know or understand. Allow him to be an individual. Realize, especially as he matures, that there may be times when you may lack the perspective of what is best for him. He may need to join the track team even though you know he has very little aptitude. Permit him to make his own decisions. Trial and error is often an important teacher.

Continually rescuing your child from suffering prevents your child the honor of learning to stand on his own. When your child stands in the face of adversity, give him the space to weather the storm. For example:

> When Colin joined a dive team, I was a little baffled. He had not previously shown any interest or aptitude in the sport. At the first diving event, I sat in anticipation. Then, gradually, my heart sank as dive after dive ended in a flop. I could hear the murmuring discomfort in the crowd. At the next match, I was stunned by a repeat performance. Though Colin spent hours practicing, subsequent matches seemed to

elicit minor improvements. The fellow parents'
sympathy was patronizing. One parent even
suggested it was cruel to let my child continue.
I sat confused, mortified for my son and myself.
I wanted to tell the fellow parents off, grab my
child, and run away. But I resisted. I sat stoic
in my pain. I held my tongue both to the fellow
parents and to my son. Colin was remarkably
relentless in his dedication. So I mentally
focused positive thoughts toward my child. He
continued to endure humiliation, match after
match. But each time he stood on the diving
board with increased determination and pride.
By the end of the season, his dives had modestly
improved, but the real value was the internal
fortitude he developed. Resisting the temptation
to rescue my child permitted him the gift of
conquering adversity. And I gave myself the gift
of honoring my instincts, trusting in my child,
and weathering fellow parents' disdain.

## Working Yourself Out of a Job

As your child develops the ability to do things for himself,
require him to do so. You may enjoy getting him up or making
his breakfast. By doing things for him that he is capable of
doing, you deny your child the capacity to gain confidence and
maturity. His future boss will not tolerate him showing up late
for work or failing to complete a project on time. There is a
learning curve for developing responsibility and self-care that
needs to be taken into account. There are the rare circumstances

when your child stayed up late for a special function and may need you to wake him or bring a forgotten report to school. Keeping these to a minimum prevents enabling. Holding your child accountable now for being ready on time, completing homework, and remembering his lunch money prepares him for adulthood. Rescuing his poor choices may make you feel valued, but it is a disservice to your child. Yelling at your child because he overslept or forgot something may make him feel bad in the moment, but it fails to teach him the lesson. Repeatedly reminding your child to do something simply makes him tune you out. Going hungry because he forgot his lunch money will teach your child to remember his lunch money faster than all the nagging, cajoling, prompting, and yelling. Certainly offer support and guidance where needed, but where he is capable, allow your child to be accountable. Expect him to be responsible. Believe in his ability. Allow your child the wisdom of experiencing the natural consequences of his behavior.

## Acceptable Risk?

You understandably want to protect your child. If he runs toward the street, you will yell for him to stop or run after him. There are times when the best way to protect your child is by allowing him to make a mistake and learn the hard way. Let's say you've told your child numerous times not to touch the stove. Yet, he stubbornly continues to insist on reaching for the hot burner. Instead of battling with him for the hundredth time, the safest, kindest act may be to allow him to touch the stove. He will quickly sense the heat and remove his hand. You will be there to administer first aid. He will have learned the danger firsthand. It may seem counterintuitive to watch your child harm himself and not stop him. And in the majority of situations this is absolutely true. On rare occasions, however, where your child is determined to ignore your warnings and where there is a controlled outcome and limited risk, allow him to learn the hard way. It may increase his confidence in your wisdom. And in the future, it will encourage him to think before acting.

One of the highest stakes and greatest potential for serious damage to self and/or property is when your child learns to drive. Future cars may drive themselves, but currently, leaning to drive is a *rite of passage* into adulthood and a true test of independence. It is also a one-ton, potentially lethal weapon. Enroll your child in the best possible driving school. Be aware of your own driving habits and the example you are setting. Establish expectations. Clarify potential consequences. Outline the responsibilities of this great privilege either in a written contract or a verbal commitment. Specify what you expect regarding treatment and maintenance of the vehicle. Establish his accountability regarding cost for insurance or fines. Discuss the use of the vehicle, curfew, errands, and any other requirements tied to his responsibility of driving, like grades or class attendance. Review the vehicle's basic maintenance (gas, oil, tire pressure, washer fluid) and where your child can find important items like the owner's manual, registration documents, and the spare tire. Stress to your child the importance of safety, the rules of the road, being a courteous driver, the risk of road rage, and respect for the law. Help your child understand the enormity of the trust you are bestowing upon him. Encourage him to honor the trust by living up to his responsibilities.

Whether it is the day your child pulls out of the driveway to drive on his own or the day he leaves home for the next phase of his life, his success will be in part because of your involvement in his life, your knowing when to step back, and your encouraging him to become a self-reliant, responsible adult. Nurturing, protecting, and guiding are all ways to help him feel safe and loved. Instilling in him the full accountability for his thoughts, feelings, and actions provides him the valuable gift of self-awareness. His ability to take full responsibility for his life and for choices that are right for him can lead to his true joy and happiness. The ultimate goal of parenting is to work yourself right out of a job. It begins with complete involvement, and then gradually, methodically you let go.

Mount Everest climbers have their commitment continuously challenged, as they progressively acclimate to the ever-increasing risks. As a parent, it is important to continually acclimate and recommit to your role. Adjust to your child's development, from being completely involved in his life to gradually relinquishing tasks and responsibilities as he gains confidence and competence. Listen carefully. Take into account the learning curve. Allow him the space to make mistakes. Celebrate as your child masters increasingly difficult tasks and gains independence.

CHAPTER 9

# Will This Never End ... Where Did the Time Go?

*Enjoy the Climb*

On a windless day, the first base camp at Mount Everest can be very hot, but by the time the climbers reach base camp four, they have endured extreme cold, high winds, crevasses, and possibly avalanches. The altitude, oxygen deprivation, and exhaustion make it a struggle for climbers to put one foot in front of the other. And as the limited window of time begins to pass, they wonder if they will ever reach the end and summit.

> I was in continual agony; I have never in my life been so tired as on the summit of Everest that day. I just sat and sat there, oblivious to everything.[10]

> —Reinhold Messner

After months of preparing, buying supplies, and readying the nursery, your baby arrives. Your emotions may run the gamut of euphoria, joy, fear, and disappointment. Whatever the initial emotion, it is generally quickly followed by sheer exhaustion brought on by interrupted nights of sleep, the demands of feeding, and the continuous changing of diapers. Simply finding time for a shower can prove overwhelming. It may feel like the all-consuming needs of your child will never end.

Then suddenly your baby sleeps through the night. He develops a routine, and you begin to regain your reserves. Just as you settle into the new schedule, teething begins and you are up again at night. You recover. Then your toddler, who was sleeping safely in his crib the night before, learns how to climb out of his crib and appears at your bedside. Around the corner are tantrums and potty training, and once again, you feel like it will never end. But these times shall also pass, as do the teacher conferences, the late-night homework projects, the bake sales, the chauffeuring all over town, the never ending expense for activities, clothes, braces, and school, and the gut-wrenching concerns about whether he is safe at a party or out driving.

## Being Present Is a Present

Each tough phase of your child's life may seem like it will never end, but they all pass. So too do the precious moments: the awe of first smiles and first steps, the tender snuggling and impromptu hugging, the sound of carefree laughter and innocent wonder, and the joyful eagerness to read a book or play a game. How to relish in the sweet moments while surviving the trials is the challenge. Continuously remind yourself whatever the immediate difficulty, it is temporary. Seek each day to slow down and create a moment to cherish with your child through a discovery, an achievement, a laugh, or a hug. Drink in the precious moments. They help you keep going in the face of another sleepless night.

> Take time to notice the good things, and the rest
> of it will seem ... manageable.
>
> —Jeremy Bangs

Keep time in perspective. Remind yourself that when he is sixteen, he will know how to use the toilet and bath himself. When he reaches sixteen, you may be dealing with his missed aim for the toilet or his resistance to a daily shower. By the time he is grown, this too shall pass.

Manage the distractions, like housework, talking on the phone, watching television, or surfing the web. Consider whether your electronics are there to support you or if you've become a slave to them. When the phone rings, do you have to answer it, or can you wait until you have finished your meal or completed your current Lego creation? Take inventory of where you spend your time. Is your time truly reflecting what you value? Each day, each and every activity is a choice. Consider whether your choices are adding value to your life.

> How you spend your time is more important than
> how you spend your money. Money mistakes
> can be corrected, but time is gone forever.[11]
>
> —David Norris

How you spend your time sends a message to your child about what you value and whether he is of value. Is watching your favorite sports team on TV more important than playing a game of catch? Does spending time jumping in the leaves come before gossiping with the neighbors? Your child is always aware of where you are and what you are doing. Think about the message you are relaying based on where you devote your time. Does he know you can be counted on to be available and be truly present?

How good are you at staying in the present moment? Are your thoughts constantly filled with the meeting you have in the morning or the bills you need to pay? Are you able to immerse yourself in the story you are reading with your child, the tower the two of you are building, or the cookies you are baking together? The activity may be filled with some moments of frustration as he learns a new task. It can also be filled with joy if you focus on the effort your child is offering and the pride he feels when he accomplishes the task. Make the characters in the story come alive. Marvel at the tower growing taller. Savor the smell of the cookies baking. These are the special moments.

You may spend hours planning a vacation or event, commemorating the moment with photographs, and envisioning the time as a special memory for your child. But it is difficult to predict which recollections will actually stand the test of time. The special trips to Disney, New York City, or the beach may fade into oblivion. And yet the unexpected family challenge of running out of gas or getting lost is recalled with fondness and laughter. Planting trees in the yard may have produced vehement complaints. However, later it is remembered with pride of accomplishment. Your purposeful statement may etch a memory. But just as likely it will be a casual comment or a moment of your less-than-stellar behavior. What you say and do speaks volumes to your child. How you spend your time conveys a special message all its own.

## Kids Do Well When Parents Are Well

Be honest with yourself about whether you are enjoying the varying stages of your child's development. You may have loved the baby stage with all the cuddling. Now you feel less connected as he begins spending more time playing with the neighborhood children. You may have been frustrated with your inability to communicate with him when he was an infant. Now you delight in his ability to express himself. The emotional and physical upheaval of puberty may seem exasperating. Or your child's emerging interests and personality may seem fascinating. Each step offers unique opportunities and blessings. Avoid holding tight to the last phase. Embrace his development and look for the wonder in his new growth.

Also consider whether you are making adequate time for yourself and your partner. Reach out to friends and relatives for support and to keep from feeling alone. Join a playgroup. Check if your local recreation center or church group has day care while you work out, volunteer, or attend a class. Manage your time while your child is napping or playing at a friend's house to include time for you to nap, read a book, have a cup of tea, take a vacation in your mind, or draw a picture. Set aside time to relax, visit, and reconnect with your partner. A strong bond with your partner is a powerful parenting tool and an important relationship when the nest is empty.

Whether you are a stay-at-home parent or work outside the home, creating balance when you feel pulled in a hundred directions is a continual challenge and, yet, an essential need.

Your physical health depends on keeping a healthy body with exercise, nutrition, and rest. Your mental health needs stimulating conversations, opportunities to learn, and time for play. Your emotional and spiritual health requires beauty, silence, inspiration, and centering. The more you incorporate these into your life, the greater the possibility that your child will emulate them and live a balanced life. Carving out large chunks of time can be unrealistic. Instead, look for five-minute increments to sit quietly alone, read a page in an interesting book, or run up and down your stairs. Take five minutes before bedtime to feel gratitude for something or some experience of the day. And then set your intentions for the next day.

Remind yourself that most of your worry and frustration is over simple inconveniences. Constantly ask yourself if $X$ is really going to matter when your child is grown. If his socks do not match or a dish is broken, is it life threatening? It may be frustrating or disappointing, but is it really worth raising your blood pressure, belittling your child, or criticizing your partner?

While routine and cleanliness play an important role in providing structure and maintaining health, balance is required. Where possible, schedule time for housework; have your partner start a load of laundry while you start the dinner. One of you folds the clothes, while the other cleans up the dishes. Include your child by making a game out of cleanup. It really is okay if the clothes are not folded to your standard. Unless you want to do all the work yourself and miss out on the fun times, you have to let go of how well some things are done at least part of the time.

## It's Only the Seventh Inning ... Hang in There

Quickly, your baby becomes a child and is off to school, and in what seems like only a moment later, he is starting to shave and has grown tall enough to look you in the eye. The more independent he becomes and the more he looks like an adult, the more challenging it becomes to stay involved in his life. His friends take center stage. He begins to challenge your belief system. He spends less and less time in your presence. It may seem like your job is done or you have little value in his life. But now, more than ever, he needs you. He needs a strong role model. He needs guidance while his brain continues to develop. He needs a safe haven when the world is cruel. He needs to know you love him and believe in him. The number of times he reaches out or accepts your offers of support may have diminished, but when he does reach, he needs you to be there.

By the teenage years, your child will work hard to push you away with arguments over everything and anything, constantly challenging your influence. He desperately wants to no longer need you. On some days he even believes you are no longer essential, but deep inside, he is scared. Have empathy. Embrace his resistance. The process helps you to begin seeing him as independent, so you too can be prepared when his time arrives to leave the nest.

## Believe

You can help your child transition to adulthood by teaching him how to make a case for what he wants and believes. Teach him how to listen to other points of view. Encourage him to seek first to understand before asking to be understood and to respect differing outlooks. Instill in him the importance of clearly stating his perspective and his needs. Remind him it is okay to agree to disagree.

Quell your own fears. Allow him to adventure off to foreign lands or attempt difficult feats. He needs to know you believe in him. Clearly set out his responsibilities, financially and otherwise. Certainly discuss ways to lessen the risk and to ensure he has thought through the necessary plans for his trek across New Zealand, his sail across the ocean, or his path to college. Assure him that if he has the passion and has done the planning, he can handle the adventure. Affirm to him he will succeed.

## A Good Kind of Pain

It may be a relief when your child leaves home, whether to college, on an adventure, or just into his own apartment. After all, the emotional tug-of-war for independence can be exhausting. And now you have time again for yourself. It may also be a time of grieving: the loss of time with your child and for your identity and role as a parent. Though the goal of parenting is to help your child become an independent adult, the pain of his leaving can feel as real as childbirth. While childbirth was painful, remember that it was a good kind of pain—it resulted in the birth of your wonderful child. Your child becoming an independent, productive person, confidently making his way in the world is a great achievement—a good kind of pain. Let the tears you shed be for joy—the joy of your child seizing the day.

As you transition to life without your child at home, remember that you are more than just a mom or dad. If you have a career or outside activities, it is helpful. If not, reevaluate what hobbies, travel, or projects you have been putting off because of the lack of time. View this change in your life as an opportunity. Instead of being an empty nester, consider yourself an open nester—open to new opportunities, to reconnecting with your partner, and to new adventures of your own.

Of course, the reality is that your role and job as a parent never really ends. It simply morphs. There may be longer stretches of time without communication. You may feel less connected. You have no idea if he is getting up and going to class or with whom he is spending time. Get on with your life, so when you do communicate with him, you have something interesting to share.

## The Invisible Awards

As your child moves to complete independence, both financially and physically, remember that he owes you nothing. He does not have to share his life with you. It is a choice. You chose to bring him into this world. It was therefore your responsibility to raise him, care for him, educate him, and provide for him to the best of your ability. Hopefully, you took the time to pause and bask in the sheer wonder and enjoyment of your child. And hopefully, through all the tough love and challenging times, you created some special moments of fun. You developed a deep relationship of respect and trust. And now he wants to continue the relationship—to spend time with you, to seek your council, and to create new special moments.

Climbing Everest is a process, not an event. A lot of it is tedious. Very little of it is glorious when you are there—that magically changes upon return. Much of the satisfaction and feeling of achievement, when it gets down to it, is very private.[12]

—Dan Holle

Much of the satisfaction and feeling of achievement from parenting is also very private. You may have moments of pride when he brings home a good grade, scores a point on a team, completes a special project, or receives awards or accolades. But the greatest pride comes when your child is grown and he tells you how much you have meant to him. The years of raising him can be full of contradictions. It may be difficult, lonely, and seem like the daily grind will never end. Before you know it, time has flown by. You yearn to hold that baby, feel him fling his arms around your legs, or watch him belly laugh. The paradox of time is how slowly it may pass in the moment but how quickly it can disappear in retrospect. Savor the sweet moments. Realize that parenting is a journey that never really ends—stay open to enjoying the climb!

CHAPTER 10

# Beyond the Summit ... Perils and Joys

## *Letting Go of the Outcome*

Climbing Mount Everest involves serious risks. The greatest perils actually exist in the hours after summiting. The climbers are fatigued. The adrenaline rush to summit has ended. The extreme cold, limited oxygen, and sheer exhaustion creeps into every cell of their bodies. The next hours will determine the climbers' fate.

As a parent, you spend a tremendous amount of time and energy caring for your child, ensuring she has a good education, and supporting her emotional development. You focus on having her become an independent adult. Finally, the day arrives. You are at the summit, attending her graduation, watching her drive away to a distant job, or walking her down the aisle. You may be filled with great joy and pride. You may feel relieved—your job is finally done! You may do a celebration dance!

Caution! Warning! Your parenting role has morphed once again! Your child has moved into the driver's seat of her own life. She is now in charge of how you fit into *her* life. Her friends and career become a priority. You are transferred to a backseat. When a spouse and child of her own enter the scene, you move to the third-row seats. You are still important. She still loves you. You are simply no longer as essential. You may continue to be a mentor, a sounding board, a safe haven, and certainly lead cheerleader. But your importance and your control has significantly shrunk. How you handle this transition will determine whether your child reaches full independence and whether your relationship continues to thrive, weakens and fades, or plummets into the abyss.

Remind yourself that her independence is a good thing. Recommit to the relationship you want to have with your child. Determine your expectations and recognize that your relationship will continue to have highs and lows. The depth of the lows will partly be determined by how well you allow her the space and time to create her own life. Will you respect her dreams and goals? How will you respond to her choices, especially the ones of which you disapprove? How will you embrace your diminishing role—as a backseat driver or by allowing her the freedom to steer her own course?

## Expectations

The summit, whether it is graduation from high school or college or reaching a certain age, conjures up expectations. What are your expectations? Is it reaching financial independence, living a particular lifestyle, getting married, owning a home, having children, serving the community, calling you daily, making choices that make you look good, or having a life that is always rosy? Do you want your child to still need you?

Do you envision your child completely independent, yet still valuing your time and counsel? Is she expected to attend a weekly dinner? Do you only want to see her at the holidays? Ask yourself, are your expectations reasonable? Have you communicated those to your child? Honesty with yourself and your child will serve you well!

## Financial Independence

Let's say your expectation is for your child to be immediately financially independent. Perhaps it will happen right away. Your child lands a good-paying dream job and is immediately self-sufficient. Just as likely, your child will have at least a few months, perhaps longer, of job searching. Her first job may be less than ideal in pay, placing limits on her financial independence. Will you continue to offer some level of monetary support as an investment in her success? If so, will you establish parameters?

Check in with yourself. Are you anxious to cut the umbilical cord in order to stabilize your own finances? Were you expecting to pay down bills, get your finances in order for retirement, or remodel your home? Maybe you've dreamed of traveling, enjoying yourself while your health is still good. After all, the clock is ticking, and your time is waning! You may also be consumed with caring for your own parents. Even if you can afford it, you may resent the continued pull on your finances. Truthfully, you want your child off your dime!

The more time that passes before your child supports herself, the more frustrated you may become. Do you take it personally? Feel inadequate? Are your friends' children having more success? Of course you want her to be self-sufficient and become successful. Sometimes the process is slower than you would prefer.

Set aside your own fears. Recognize that she feels frustrated, overwhelmed, and even afraid. She wants to do well. She wants your assistance but feels like a failure for needing it. She is embarrassed. She is a grown-up and is supposed to be able to handle this. Have compassion. Reinforce your confidence in her. Express your pride in even the smallest steps toward success. Your belief in her will do more to promote her than any ranting.

At the same time, if you are paying for some or all of her bills, you have a right to understand her plan of action. You can help mitigate her defensiveness by clearly defining your boundaries and expectations. For example, you will provide assistance until a certain date or provide a specific amount of money. In return, will you require help with chores, or she is responsible for her own laundry? Figure out your needs and your limits. The clearer these boundaries are outlined, the more she can focus on what she needs to do. She will feel more empowered, and you will both feel less resentful.

As your child reaches financial stability, will you continue to pay for her cell phone, her vacations? She may naturally be upset and resist you pulling the plug. Who doesn't enjoy the gravy train? In her eyes, you are adding an unnecessary burden to her. It may be painful to face her disappointment. Do you want her to stay indebted to you? If you continue support where she is capable, are you allowing her to develop full independence? Will you become resentful at the sustained pull on your finances? Having to tighten her budget and assume full responsibility may be uncomfortable for her in the short term. Ultimately, she will feel more accomplished and empowered.

Now let's say your child is financially independent. Yay! You feel proud and relieved, so you begin booking your trip to Bermuda. But wait. How is she managing her money? Has she set up savings and retirement accounts? Is she spending every last dime frivolously? Are her choices any of your business? Do you wonder what will become of her if her job vanishes? Will she expect you to bail her out of trouble? Will you? Have you clearly discussed your boundaries? Do your actions support your words? If you are constantly doling out money, she may presume that you are her safety net. Sometimes it is difficult to step back and watch your child do with a little less and struggle to make ends meet. Remember that the process can be a valuable lesson and teach her real self-sufficiency.

### Just Hello

Your child has been on her own for several months. The few times she has called have been to ask for money or complain about a roommate or boss. Today she called just to say hello. She asks how things are going with you. You keep waiting for the request, the complaint, but it doesn't come. She genuinely wants to know about your life. She called simply to make a connection with you. Oh, the incredible joy!

### Life Choices

Your child is off successfully living her life. She has a good-paying job and is establishing her financial independence. You are so proud! Then you find out she is making lifestyle choices you do not agree with. She has moved in with a less-than-desirable boyfriend or is spending her free time partying. Your fear for her and your disappointment in her choices can cause a serious strain in your relationship. Take a big, deep breath. Your words and actions will have lasting implications.

Your child has the right to make her own decisions. She has the right to make her own mistakes. To you, her choices may seem immature, impulsive, or dangerous. Can you remember when you were her age? Were all of your decisions wise? You have many years of experience, but she is just beginning the journey. You want to protect her. You want to infuse her with the knowledge you've obtained through the years, to shield her from pain and suffering. The challenge: experience is often the most effective teacher.

If you push, demand, or attempt emotional blackmail, your child will likely reject any advice. She may certainly avoid being honest with you in the future. She may even continue her behavior just to prove you wrong. Like most young adults, she is convinced she knows it all. She believes that she is invincible.

Let your child know you love her even if you do not approve of or agree with all of her actions. Calmly, matter-of-factly, explain what it is that you fear. Let her know your boundaries and the support you are willing to offer if she needs you. Then, trust it will work out. It may seem your child is too close to the edge of danger, but perhaps she is actually safely inspecting the surroundings. The path from your vantage point looks like she is on the crumbling edge of the cliff. In reality, she may be a safe distance from the brink. Even if it turns out to be the rocky edge and the consequences of your child's actions end in painful results, trust her! Trust that it will work out. It is hard, but your child has the right to live her life her way.

If you want to maintain an open, honest relationship, you have to respect your child's decisions. Allow her the space to make mistakes, explore the world at large, and find her place. Can you do that? Can you accept her? Forgive her? Can you forgive yourself if your child is not perfect? It is soooo hard to let go and allow your child the right to her own opinions, decisions, and lifestyle. But it is necessary! And in the end, your willingness to respect your child's choices will encourage her to be more open to considering your opinion.

## My Treat

Your child calls and suggests you go to a movie together. After looking over the options, you narrow it down and arrive at the theater. You pull out your wallet to pay. Your child says, "I'll pay—my treat." Your heart stops. You hold back the tears. Your feel overwhelmed with pride and gratitude.

## A Down Day

Your child is off making her way in the world. Last week she sounded great—her job was going well, and she was looking forward to a beach weekend with friends. Today she calls practically in tears. Her car has broken down, and life in general is looking bleak. Your heart sinks. You want to scrape her up off the floor and hold her in your arms. You want to magically repair her car and bring out the sunshine. Slow yourself down. Assess the situation. Does she want advice or just to vent? Is she confused about the process of who to contact for the repair? If so, walk her through the process. Is she frustrated by the events of the day? If so, listen.

You may be tempted to send her money—buy away her pain. But unless she is in serious need of the money, allow her to handle the stress. Dealing with these challenges is part of the maturing process. Exude compassion. Assure her that she can handle the situation. It may be uncomfortable to know she is having a bad day, because her pain is your pain. It feels better to believe her life is rosy! Be grateful she wants you to be a sounding board when life is tough. Even if she appreciates your suggestions, be okay with her choosing a different option. Give her permission to figure out the solution. Reassure her that she can resolve the problem.

## The Card

It is your birthday. You receive the typical obligatory phone call from your child. You are grateful. It is good to hear her voice. Later in the day you go to the mailbox. She sent a card. You are touched by her thoughtfulness. You begin to read the card. It is short, but the words are from her heart. She appreciates you in her life! The flood gates open until you are nothing more than a puddle on the floor.

## Confidence

Your child has been at her job for a couple of years. It pays the bills. It allows her to travel and pay for her new car. So you figure she is happy. Then one day your child calls and tells you how much she hates her job. Her boss is an ogre. She is miserable. She feels stuck. She has bills and obligations. For a moment you are frozen, confused. You knew this was not your child's dream job, but you had no idea she was this unhappy. Are her expectations unrealistic? Does she lack confidence in her ability to make a change? Is she allowing herself to learn from the ugly gifts of her boss? Take a deep breath! Is your child venting? Does she need a cheerleader? Is she seeking advice?

Listen. Then consider reminding your child of all the skills she has learned in the past two years on the job, of how valuable those skills will be to another company, of the courage she has exhibited in leaving the nest and making it on her own, and of how responsible she has been. Tell her how proud you are of her.

If your child seeks more, let her know it is okay to look for another job. (Encourage her to keep the current job until she finds a new one, as it is much is easier to find a job when you have a job.) Ask your child to contemplate what work would make her happy, what she likes about her current employment, and what seems to be lacking. Help her center herself and explore options. Allow her to determine what choices she has and what steps to take. Your child may just be having a down day and need a reminder of her strengths. Or she may actually feel trapped and need a reminder of her value and of the importance of her own thoughts in creating her life.

## The Gift

The holidays tend to involve lots of gifts for your child. This year your child hands you a gift, beautifully wrapped. It has a touching card. Inside is a unique gift from her business travels a few months prior. You soak in the knowledge that during her trip, your child thought of you. She took the time to find a gift she knew you would enjoy. You feel loved, cherished. You are overwhelmed by your child's generosity and thoughtfulness.

## The Significant Other

Your child brings home the serious boyfriend. Hopefully you love him. They seem to bring out the best in one another. He is respectful, has a good job, and appears to be crazy about your child—yay! You are excited but also apprehensive. Is he actually good enough for your child? What does he think of you?

If they are talking about marriage, what is their financial expectation of you regarding the wedding? How will marriage affect the limited time you have with your child, especially regarding holidays and vacations? Your heart is torn. Part of you is thrilled your child has found someone to share her life with—someone who is kind and makes her happy. Another part of you feels your significance further diminishing. Oh, there will be times your child still calls to ask your advice, share her day's events, or just say hello, but she will now need you even less. She has someone else to lean on, to share with. Remember—this is the very thing you hoped for. It is another good pain.

Welcome this new addition. Embrace the joy he brings your child. Commit to honoring their time and boundaries. And consider the following:

Thomas, my kindergartener, invited his best friend, Emma, over to play. Emma and I stood in the yard waiting for Thomas to get the bubbles from the garage. Emma turned and said, "Tom and I had fun at school today."

I replied, "That's great! By the way, his name is Thomas not Tom."

Emma put her hands on her hips, looked me in the eye, and said matter-of-factly, "He told me I could call him Tom, so I will."

I had just experienced my first lesson in how to be an in-law.

The relationship between your child and her significant other is theirs, not yours. Certainly encourage premarital counseling. But unless there is something seriously amiss, like abuse, be slow to offer your opinion. It is their life, and they have the right to live it their way. If you show them respect, they will do the same for you and will be much more welcoming of you in their lives.

## The Project

Your child calls to check in and see how things are going. You mention your summer plans to remove some old, overgrown landscaping. She says to let her know when, and she will take vacation time to come and help. Your voice catches. You tell her that would be great. As you hang up the phone, you are overwhelmed by love. The challenges of child rearing have suddenly melted away, and all you can now feel is blessed.

## Attitude

Whether it is how to work the latest gadget, understand the newest slang, or keep up on current fashion, your child can be a great resource of knowledge. Asking for your child's advice empowers her and acknowledges that she has something to contribute. On another level, it is recognition of your vulnerability and the shift of power within the relationship. Your child may find it humorous that you need assistance. She may find it enjoyable to help you. Other times your child may be annoyed or disappointed. This is especially evident if she feels burdened or believes you need to take more personal responsibility in staying current. The result may be a condescending attitude.

Assess whether you are leaning too much on your child. Is the information or assistance available in other ways? Do you need to take more responsibility for your own learning? Regardless, it is important to let your child know if her attitude has become patronizing. Be open to allowing her to air her frustration. Listen. Work on improving your own behavior while also requiring your child to remain respectful.

## Celebrate

Mount Everest climbers are exhausted as they reach the summit. Their satisfaction at the peak is brief. They need to quickly turn their focus to the treacherous descent. Your child reaching the summit of adulthood may be exciting and fulfilling. It can also be exhausting and full of bewildering challenges. You may have anticipated your child waking up at the summit all wise, mature, and grateful only to realize the process is actually slower and more gradual.

As your child becomes self-sufficient, set your boundaries. Examine your expectations. Yes, at times you may feel like the abandoned chair sitting in the corner, or a part of you may be in panic mode. How will I protect her? How do I make sure she makes the right decisions? The reality is you cannot. You will continue to be dismayed at some of your child's decisions and wonder where you went wrong. Get over it! Forgive yourself and your child for being less than perfect. Trust that your child is capable of handling her responsibilities—her own life. Continue to encourage her to nurture herself, forgive herself, and visualize what she wants her life to look like. Empower your child by believing in her, even as you watch her stumble. Allow her the honor of pursuing her own path. Know she can and will be okay.

In those times when you feel discarded, get on with your life. Concentrate on becoming the ever improving, best version of yourself. Remind yourself that your child still loves you. She still appreciates your approval, your accolades, and, at times, even your advice. Bask in the moments your child shares with you. Focus your intention and attention on the relationship you want to create. Maintain awe at the wonder of your child's uniqueness. Be grateful for and cherish the continued opportunity to be in your child's life!

# Afterword

I received a phone call—the kind every parent prays deep inside will never happen.

"Your son has been shot." The hospital attendant kept repeating the message, but I kept thinking it had to be a prank—a very cruel prank. I was hearing the words, but my mind and heart would not accept the reality. I felt as if the ground beneath me had been sucked away.

My son was more than 1,600 miles away. The attendant could only tell me he was alive—not his condition or prognosis, not what had happened, only that he was in a hospital all alone.

My son had recently moved, and I did not know his roommates' names or how to reach them. Dawn was hours away. It would be late afternoon before I could reach my son. I desperately wanted someone to be at his side. I was frantic for help, so I posted about the situation on Facebook. Within a short time, word spread across the country. My son's friends and roommates began arriving at the hospital. I felt solace in knowing he was no longer alone.

On the flight, my thoughts became a battlefield. Part of me was bursting with anger and revenge. I wanted the person responsible to be tortured and destroyed. Another part of me knew the hatred would eat my soul. I could best help my son by forgiving the perpetrator and moving forward.

When I finally arrived at the hospital and walked into ICU, the frontline was on full display. My son lay in the bed hooked up to tubes and in immense pain, his body and emotions battered. Standing beside him were angels dressed in friends' clothing and medical attire.

Recovery was littered with backslides and miracles, but my son did make a full recovery. As often happens, a crisis evoked a plethora of blessings. Love and support poured in from family, friends, and strangers. My soul was buoyed, and my heart began to heal, soften.

I began to contemplate the young man who had shot my son. I wondered whether he had grown up feeling loved and appreciated and whether his parents had the knowledge they needed to guide him. I had been blessed with many mentors and opportunities. It was time to share the wisdom. This book is my hope for more enlightened parents, more empowered kids, and a kinder world.

# A Brief Summary of Mount Everest

Mount Everest lies between Tibet China and Nepal in Asia's Himalayan range. At higher than 29,000 feet above sea level, rising almost five and a half miles into the sky, it is considered the highest mountain on Earth. It is shaped like a three-sided pyramid, with its sides coved in glaciers and ice. Although not considered the most technical mountain to climb, Mount Everest is one of the most challenging.

Because of its high altitude, there is decreased atmospheric pressure and therefore diminished air to breath. Breathing itself can become exhausting. Reduced oxygen in the blood can result in it taking twelve hours to travel little more than a mile. The extreme cold, high winds, avalanches, rock falls, and hazards of slipping and falling all add to the danger. The highest regions are referred to as the Death Zone. Rescue by helicopter is generally impractical. Fellow climbers are usually struggling to function themselves. The magnitude and multitude of these factors makes injury at this level life threatening. More than two hundred climbers, an average of one in ten, have died. Because of the extreme conditions, most of the corpses remain on the mountain.

Expeditions generally occur in the limited window of time during the months of April and May, before the monsoon season. During this time, the change in jet stream helps to reduce the hurricane-force winds. Expeditions follow one of two routes—the southeast ridge or the north ridge. Completion takes forty to sixty days. It involves alternating hikes and rest at preset camps to gradually acclimate. Without sufficient acclimation, the reduced oxygen in the blood can cause dizziness, nausea, confusion, and weakness. And in severe cases, it can lead to brain swelling, fluid in the lungs, and death.

In addition to the great physical risk, climbing Mount Everest is an expensive endeavor. Hiring guides and porters and obtaining the necessary permits and gear can easily exceed $50,000.

The first recorded summit of Mount Everest occurred on May 29, 1953, by the New Zealander Edmund Hillary and Tenzing Norgay, a Sherpa from Nepal. Sherpas are mountain climbing guides and porters originally from the Himalayas. They are highly regarded for their knowledge of the mountain and exceptional endurance at high altitude.

In Nepal, Mount Everest is honored as *Sagarmāthā*, or Goddess of the Sky. In Tibet, it is revered as *Qomolangma*, or Holy Mother.

The sheer challenge, essential preparation, and laser focus required for climbing Mount Everest offers great analogies to the adventure of parenting.

# Acknowledgments

I want to express profound appreciation to Pat Palmieri for her contributions. She spent numerous hours discussing, recommending, and editing—thank you!

Deep gratitude also goes out to the following individuals whose wisdom and talents further enriched this book:

Jillian Sullivan's reflective viewpoint as a PhD research analyst offered breadth and affirmation. Carolanne Roberts shared her editing expertise. Stefanie Ramirez and Rebecca Guarino brought new mom outlooks, while Beth Sullivan and Karen Lilley offered considerations from further along the path. Luke Gaeckle contributed his esteemed feedback and editing talent.

Pam Prince Eason shared insights as an acclaimed, respected business woman extraordinaire and remarkable individual. Karen Lowy leant constructive criticism, astute assistance, and valued friendship. Karen Jones added heartfelt enthusiasm and deeply treasured support. Barbara Riley provided her distinctive perspectives and cherished care.

The books and/or life messages of Dr. Wayne Dyer, Dr. Deepak Chopra, Louise Hay, Oprah Winfrey, and Carole O'Connell provided inspiration and guidance.

Many other mentors, friends, family, and passing acquaintances have blessed my life and therefor this book with their wisdom.

Thank you to the writers and poets who shared their words with the world and granted reprint approval.

To my husband, Steve Gaeckle, you add richness to my life with laughter and wisdom. Your love and support continuously lift my spirit. Andrew and Ethan Gaeckle, you amaze me, inspire me, and fill me with joy. Thank you for the honor of being your mom.

# Notes

1  Wheatley, Margaret. http://margaretwheatley.com/, comment on Disturb Me, Please! *The Works: Your Source to Being Fully Alive*, Summer 2000.

2  Weathers, Beck and Stephen G. Michaud *Left For Dead*, Villard Books, a division of Penguin Random House 2000 ISBN978-0-375-50588-1.

3  Gibran, Kahlil. *The Prophet*, New York: Alfred A. Knopf, 1923, Oneworld Publications 1998 ISBN 1-85168-178-7.

4  Dr. Steve Maraboli. http://www.stevemaraboli.com/

5  Harper Todd, Susan. http://www.womenhavevision.com

6  Fulghum, Robert. *Uh-Oh: Some Observations from Both Sides of the Refrigerator Door*. Ballentine Books, Ivy Books 1993 Penguin Random House ISBN 0-679-40103-2 pgs 145-6.

7  Cited in https://en.wikipedia.org/wiki/Edmund_Hillary; McKinlay, Tom (24 May 2006). "Wrong to Let Climber Die, says Sir Edmund." *The New Zealand Herald*. Retrieved 29 September 2011.

8  Cited in https://en.wikipedia.org/wiki/Lincoln_Hall_(climber).

9  Roughton, Ralph. Retired psychoanalyst, former director of the Emory University Psychoanalytic Institute and author.

10  Cited in "Reinhold Messner." *Encyclopædia Britannica. Encyclopædia Britannica Online*. Encyclopædia Britannica Inc., 2015. Web. 04 Mar. 2015. http://www.britannica.com/

EBchecked/topic/377230/Reinhold-Messner;    Messner,
Reinhold; *Everest: Expedition zum Endpunkt* (1978; *Everest:
Expedition to the Ultimate.*

[11] Norris, David. Irish Parliament Senator and author. http://
senatordavidnorris.ie/

[12] Holle, Dan. http://danholle.com/perrysfield/evrest.shtml,
commented on Long-Way-From-Home-Page, *The 1994
American Everest Expedition or ... How I Spent My Summer
Vacation.*

# References

1. Werner, K. and J.J. Gross. Emotion Regulation and Psychopathology: A Conceptual Framework. (2010).
2. Schroeder, S. A. "We Can Do Better: Improving the Health of the American People." *New England Journal of Medicine* 357, 1221-1228, doi:doi:10.1056/NEJMsa073350 (2007).
3. Tangney, J. P., R.F. Baumeister, and A.L. Boone. "High Self-Control Predicts Good Adjustment, Less Pathology, Better Grades, and Interpersonal Success." *Journal of Personality* 72, 271-324 (2008).
4. Duckworth, A. L. and M.E.P. Seligman. "Self-Discipline Outdoes IQ in Predicting Academic Performance of Adolescents." *Psychological Science* 16, 939-944 (2005).
5. Mischel, W., E.B. Ebbesen, and A. Raskoff Zeiss. "Cognitive and Attentional Mechanisms in Delay of Gratification." *Journal of Personality and Social Psychology* 21, 204 (1972).
6. Shoda, Y., W. Mischel, and P.K. Peake. "Predicting Adolescent Cognitive and Self-Regulatory Competencies from Preschool Delay of Gratification: Identifying Diagnostic Conditions." *Developmental Psychology* 26, 978 (1990).
7. Mischel, W., Y. Shoda, and P.K. Peake. "The Nature of Adolescent Competencies Predicted by Preschool Delay

of Gratification." *Journal of Personality and Social Psychology* 54, 687 (1988).

8. Eisenberg, N., R.A. Fabes, and T.L. Spinrad. *Handbook of Child Psychology: Social, Emotional, and Personality Development* (ed N. Eisenberg) (Wiley Online Library, 2006).

9. De Wolff, M. S. and M.H. van Ijzendoorn. "Sensitivity and Attachment: A Meta-Analysis on Parental Antecedents of Infant Attachment." *Child Development* 68, 571-591, doi:10.1111/j.1467-8624.1997.tb04218.x (1997).

10. Stams, G.-J. J. M., F. Juffer, and M.H. van Ijzendoorn. "Maternal Sensitivity, Infant Attachment, and Temperament in Early Childhood Predict Adjustment in Middle Childhood: The Case of Adopted Children and Their Biologically Unrelated Parents." *Developmental Psychology* 38, 806-821, doi:10.1037/0012-1649.38.5.806 (2002).

11. Leerkes, E. M., A. Nayena Blankson, and M. O'Brien. "Differential Effects of Maternal Sensitivity to Infant Distress and Nondistress on Social-Emotional Functioning." *Child development* 80, 762-775, doi:10.1111/j.1467-8624.2009.01296.x (2009).

12. Aunola, K. and J.E. Nurmi. "The Role of Parenting Styles in Children's Problem Behavior." *Child Development* 76, 1144-1159, doi:10.1111/j.1467-8624.2005.00840.x-i1 (2005).

13. Nofziger, S. "The 'Cause' of Low Self-Control." *Journal of Research in Crime and Delinquency* 45, 191-224, doi:10.1177/0022427807313708 (2008).

14. Vohs, K. D. and R.F. Baumeister. *Handbook of Self-Regulation, Second Edition: Research, Theory, and Applications.* (Guilford Publications, 2010).

15. Augustine, A. A. S.H. Hemenover. "On the Relative Effectiveness of Affect Regulation Strategies: A

Meta-Analysis." *Cognition & Emotion* 23, 1181-1220, doi:10.1080/02699930802396556 (2009).

16. Hajcak, G. and S. Nieuwenhuis. "Reappraisal Modulates the Electrocortical Response to Unpleasant Pictures." *Cognitive, Affective, & Behavioral Neuroscience* 6, 291-297, doi:10.3758/cabn.6.4.291 (2006).

17. Holzel, B. K. *et al.* "Mindfulness Practice Leads to Increases in Regional Brain Gray Matter Density." *Psychiatry Research: Neuroimaging* 191, 36-43 (2011).

18. Beddoe, A. E. and S.O. Murphy. "Does Mindfulness Decrease Stress and Foster Empathy among Nursing Students?" *The Journal of Nursing Education* 43, 305-312 (2004).

19. Grossman, P., L. Niemann, S. Schmidt, and H. Walach." Mindfulness-Based Stress Reduction and Health Benefits: A Meta-Analysis." *Journal of Psychosomatic Research* 57, 35-44 (2004).

# About the Author

Carole E. Gaeckle teaches Emotional Intelligence and Critical Decision-Making Skills and supports Restorative

Justice Practices for The Conflict Center in Denver, Colorado. She previously worked in the corporate world, owned her own business, and served as a counselor at a juvenile detention facility. Carole has a passion for inspiring people to become the best version of themselves, to live their best lives, and to reach their potential.

Carole graduated from the University of Tennessee and has two grown children. She resides in Colorado with her husband where she enjoys camping, hiking, skiing, and an occasional high adventure.